Looking
Back Through
The Life Of The
Master Artist

DOROTHY SLIKKER

Looking Back Through The Life Of The Master Artist

READERSMAGNET, LLC

Looking Back Through The Life Of The Master Artist
Copyright © 2018 by Dorothy Slikker

Published in the United States of America
ISBN Paperback: 978-1-947765-88-7
ISBN eBook: 978-1-947765-89-4

All rights reserved. No part of this publication may be reproduced, stored in a retrieval system or transmitted in any way by any means, electronic, mechanical, photocopy, recording or otherwise without the prior permission of the author except as provided by USA copyright law.

No lines, parts, and quotations were taken from other books or any previous publications.

The opinions expressed by the author are not necessarily those of ReadersMagnet, LLC.

ReadersMagnet, LLC
10620 Treena Street, Suite 230 | San Diego, California, 92131 USA
1.619. 354. 2643 | www.readersmagnet.com

Book design copyright © 2018 by ReadersMagnet, LLC. All rights reserved.
Cover design by Ericka Walker
Interior design by Shieldon Watson

DEDICATION

I WANT TO DEDICATE this book first of all to my wonderful husband and partner through life. Without the support from John I would not be an artist let alone have all of the opportunities that crossed my path in the pursuit of my goals. A lot of the things that came my way were because John encouraged me to push forward towards them and gave me the confidence to manage all that came to me. He provided a wonderful home, family and love, to you, "John William Slikker Jr." I dedicate my life and book with all the love and pride I can muster from my soul.

In this dedication I would like to bring forward my Grandparents Charles Delbert and Amelia Ann Searcy without their journey to California during the Dust Bowl of the 1930's I would not have existed.

Mom and Willard Sanders gave me life for which I hope I have lived in a way that would have made them proud of me.

Bill Shultz I do thank you for giving me a new lease on life by marring my mother Mary, giving me a whole new way of life to live. Without your guiding hand I may not have made the decisions that led me into the direction my life held for me. Once again I say thank you for two wonderful sisters that you added in my life, I have to admit Beverly made it interesting. As of today Beverly and I are the only two children left in this wonderful generation of people of this amazing family.

INTRODUCTION

This story will tell you the about the life of Dorothy Sanders Slikker. Who she is and how she got to the place of being an artist, from her first humble beginnings to her life at the present time.

Dorothy is the product of life in the 1950's. A time when a child actually did as she was told and did not try to buck the system as the punishment was way too harsh to bear in this time of life. A child was to be seen and not heard.

I tell you about the stories I heard while growing up about the dust bowl and what it was like to make the farmers in Oklahoma move to California in the 1930's. The uncontrollable dust and the deaths of so many children and the farmers losing their farms because they could not grow the crops and the winds blew all of the top soil away and made it impossible to produce. This led them to lose everything and caused them to load up and make this trip into the unknown.

After arriving in California came the enormous task of finding a home place, a place to put down your roots. Farmers have to have a place of permanence. Next came finding work to take care of the family, this became a family task as all moneys would be pooled for the purpose of survival. Families would work together in the fields for this purpose. This whole movement became known as the migration of the Okies.

My mother getting married at the age of 14 and having three babies by the age of 17. This was not an unknown thing to do at this time of the 1940's

World War 11 and the bombing of Pearl Harbor, all of the families being separated during the war, a lot of the families being broken because of death or divorce caused by the war.

My mother remarried his name was Bill Shultz his family was in the farming business and I acquired two more sisters, Beverly and Judy. Life went on and it became a story of making yours and mine, ours. This they managed the best they could and we stayed together for the rest of the life of the family.

College and marriage for Dorothy to another farmer his name was John Slikker. This was the one thing I did not want to do was marry a farmer. John was my best friend and encouraged my art career and helped me all the way. He encouraged my passion.

Making the Top 60 INTERNATIONA CONTEMPORARY MASTERS was such an honor for me but when I also made the WW TOP 100 WORLD CONTEMPORARY MASTERS I was beside myself. I was so proud that I sat down and wrote my first book

MY ARTWALK to the CONTEMPORARY MASTERS.

I hope you read my story and can see what it does for one to reach a goal that was set by herself in her young life.

I am now starting to paint and write my second art book look for it next year.

LET'S START WITH THE Dust Bowl of Oklahoma, this is a time of trial for the Searcy family (Charles Delbert Searcy) being farmers and having their lively hood blown away. This is how the story was passed down by my grandmother (Amelia Ann Clary) and I hope you can get the feeling of the ugliness that went with the storm and families. My grandmother (granny) couldn't keep the dirt out of the food or clothes the children wore and the land had become so barren that my grandpa couldn't make the crops and there for could not pay for the loans that come with farming. Along with the rest of the community, after the last black cloud of dust swarmed and killed a few children, grandpa and granny loaded the family and belongings and headed for California. Having been a farmer and worked for himself, leaving was a hard decision to make. Now no money, job or a way of making a living he was driving to California and the unknown. Along with the rest of the migration they became known as "Okies" if a black person thinks he was scorned, they should have had a taste of what the okies had to endure. In Oklahoma they were prestigious and in California they were a threat to the citizens who felt that the okies were taking all of the jobs. Grandpa went from a land owner to a farm labourer.

Charles Delbert age 15

Load of potatoes near Shafter, CA.

Granpa Charles Delbert

Charles Dorothy and Ruby Sanders we are now living with granny and grandpa

Uncle Billy Wesley Redwine and Uncle Jack

When they reached California they were taken advantage of just like all of the rest of the okies, a contractor would get them work in the fields and then take all of their money but 10%. They would stay in labor camps, which they felt was great, until they tried to leave and then they would be beaten or murdered and the family held hostage. It was hard for them to escape, they did just that. Losing all the money they had earned.

As they travelled into California, they soon came to the San Joaquin Valley, known as the bread basket of the world. They joined the mass of transient farm labour's following the crop harvest. A lot of the people coming to California stopped and made their homes in the farming community of Lamont. Today the community holds a festival honouring the Okie's that stayed and built futures there for their families. Farming was the only work Grandpa had ever done. In 1934 they travelled to the town of Shafter and managed to acquire a couple of lots. Grandpa and Uncle Billy and Uncle Jack put up a Tent and started preparing the second lot for the garden to grow their vegetables for the winter. He planted fruit trees and berry vines for making canned fruit and jelly for the corn bread one of their main meal breads. Granny prepared all of the meals from scratch and stretching the food with the main staple on every okie's table pinto beans and corn bread, potatoes, sliced onions if there was meat they had gravy to stretch it around. To this day I can see my grandpa stirring his honey and butter to get it soft enough for the cornbread. Grandpa continued to look for work by the day and worked when he found something they wanted him to do. The family had to go on welfare; this would last until the first member of the family found employment. Uncle Billy and Uncle Jack got a job delivering newspapers and the family had to give up their welfare, which was fine as they had no intention to have government help. It was hard to make ends meet on these wages. Being fugal and having no frills the family managed to get by. Speaking about granny she could never turn down one of her meals meager as they would be, to a stranger. While they were still in Oklahoma a gang that had pretty boy Floyd as a member held up a Bank. In those days the criminals would steal from the rich and give it to the poor. To make a long story short pretty boy Floyd was on the run and happened to stop at grannies, she prepared him a meal and harboured him for a short time. Not long after he was shot by the police. Today she still tells her story with a smile of satisfaction on her face for doing her part. All of the poor people thought of them as heroes since they always came when someone was in need. A lot of the time you could catch granny in deep thought and ask what she was thinking about, she answered the dust you just couldn't get it out of the house as it would come through the cracks. You just seemed to be smothering in it. All those children and she would shed a tear remembering what had happened not so long ago.

On the lot they lived in a tent until Grandpa could find employment on a farm in Delano picking cotton. Oh the stories that I grew up listening to. They put Grandpa in the center of the field to pick cotton and he would have to pick just part way out, if he got too close to the end of the field he risked getting shot. The people didn't like the Okies taking their jobs. Grandpa kept

Granny in the striped shirt and Mary next to her with the glasses on Potato shed crew 1946

looking for work in the farms around Shafter. Jack Sill hired him and kept him working until he retired at the age of 72. As grandpa got older Mr. Sill made it his job to be the irrigator and he would work at night so that he didn't have to fight the heat. Grandpa had his unique way of keeping time so that he didn't let the water get away from him. One way was to lie down in the field the water would wake him up, and when it was just a short run for the water he would light a cigarette when it burned to his fingers it would wake him. When it was time for him to retire and started to receive his Social Security checks he would not cash them as he said he didn't need government help. It was hard to convince him it was money he earned. None the less he didn't cash a check for about a year.

After a couple of years in the tent they had saved enough money to build a four room house. While Grandpa went to work Granny, the boys, and my mother Mary Geneva built the house. The boys dug the hole for the outhouse and Granny built it, it was a one holler. I also remember them digging a big hole just outside the back door, it was the cesspool and leach lines for the house big enough if they ever got a bath room.

Uncle Billy and Lois

They did a wonderful job on the house, it had running water (no hot water) granny had a sink and grandpa had a table and bowl for washing up and shaving, he also had a nail to hang his leather shaving strap, there was a stove, cabinets and a kitchen table. The wires were all exposed and laid next to the ceiling, open light bulbs no fixtures; they lived there until their deaths in 1984. The house was about as primitive as you could build it in the 30's no insulation in the walls, just paint and wall paper. You entered through the living room door, went through the bedroom into the kitchen, there would be grandpa saying wait a minute and then display with his hands that your butt was two axe handles wide. There was another room off to the side that mama and her brothers shared. Life was hard and there was just a token bit of help from the government (welfare) it ended when the first member of the family got a job. Granny was a woman that never complained about anything that came her way. She was content with her lot in life and raised a happy family, she had a hard working man and kids that had a heart of gold they would help anyone in need of their help. Labour was often the only thing they could offer and more times than not that was all that was needed, a helping hand.

Like all the rest of the family mama (Mary Geneva) went to the fields and picked up potatoes. In the crew there was another family, two girls and five boys (The Sanders Family) Mother and her friend Martha caught the eyes of two of the Sanders boys Homer and Willard. Mary fell hard in love and managed to get her parents to let her marry Willard, she was only 14yrs. old by the time she reached the ripe old age of 17 Mary had three children Ruby, Dorothy, and Charles. My Indian heritage is through my father. His mother's sister was the white child that was kidnapped by the Indians, as she grew older she became the bride of the chief. One of her children was Kahwana Parker he carried his mother's maiden name. He was the famous Indian that worked with Abraham Lincoln to get the Apache Chief Geronimo to the reservation in Florida, promising them that at a later date they would be

Louis Ruby Charles Dorothy and Donnie Sanders

Mary Dorothy Willard and Ruby Sanders

returned to their own lands. It never happened. His mother was set free to live as a white woman, but she could not survive in the white world and went back to the reservation, taking her children with her.

Mary Sanders

After Mary and Willard married life didn't change much for Mary, she still had to work in the fields and potato sheds, the only difference was the burden of the small children. Ruby was born on June 7th, 1939 in Bakersfield, Ca. and I Dorothy Mae was born on Dec.1, 1940, Charles came along in Sept 21, 1942. As you might say we were the first California Born Oakies as Buck Owens sang in one of his songs. The first part of my recall was being taken to the fields along with mom and playing by the sacks of potatoes all day and helping to pull the vines from the freshly dug potatoes, it seems as though I still can smell the dirt that was freshly turned with the fresh potatoes. You know the smell of wet dirt after a small shower.

Dec.7th 1941 was the most terrifying day in the lives of all Americans, the day of the bombing of Pearl Harbor and the beginning of WW11 for the United States of America. Most all of the able bodied men in the USA loaded up to go and serve the

USA and help to protect our country and loved ones. The men left for the war effort, leaving the women to fend for the family. Like some families that had a few boys they all joined the same service. Daddy had four brothers and they all joined the Marines. This family was one of the lucky ones that did not lose any of the brothers in battle. After the brothers that were on the same ship lost their lives the service separated the family of boys so that a family couldn't lose all of them in the war at the same time. Dad's brothers were in different parts of the war. Daddy was in the war in the Philippines. He was gone for most of the duration of the war. As I recall there was this young man that was at our house, he was showing us tricks like putting a bean in one ear and it would come out of the other ear. When I was along I tried this well it didn't come out so I got a stick and poked the bean through my eardrum. After a while it started to sprout and cause pain, mom rushed me to the Dr. and to this day I can still feel the pain of them digging it out of my ear, this left me deft in the right ear. Many years later Uncle Billy told me it was not a stranger that showed me the bean trick it was my father Willard, not thinking that I would try it later on my own. Over the years I would have two or three operations on the ear leaving me with a mastoid ear. Being away from his family Willard was unfaithful and so was Mary. This goes to show that absence does not makes the heart grow fonder. Like most families the war caused families to break up. Our father Willard told mama to get a divorce as he had remarried. Our cousin and my half-brother both told me that he told them that when he came home from the war, he found mama with another man. It looks like both sides have a story to tell. What I know is that he never came to visit or send me a birthday card. He could have forgotten when it was my birthday, but everyone in the world knows when it Christmas time. As far as I was concerned he was out of my life and I considered him as dead.

Ruby and Charles went to live with him as they reached their teens. I never gave in and considered that he was gone from my life forever. One day while I was at work in my shop he called my home and told my oldest son Jon he was Grandpa Sanders, when I got home from work my son asked "mama who is Grandpa Sanders"? I had never spoken of him to my children, they didn't know he existed, thus I had to sit down and explain this painful part of my life. As a small child I remember living in labour camps and different migrant camps. There are stories that Ruby and I tried to help our mother with the house work and mopping the whole living quarters with cold greasy dish water. I also can recall the breaking into of our apartment by a disgruntled suitor of our mother when we lived in Myricks Corner. After this event, we moved into my grannies wash house. Mary and the kids lived there in the wash house and ate in the main house. I remember Uncle Billy and Uncle Jack building a wall to make a room out of wood studs and card board boxes. Mama and Charles slept in one room and Ruby and I shared the other. Life was so simple then, any way it was heaven being able to have granny with us all the time. Granny made our clothes out of chicken feed, and flour sacks. The material in the sacks served us well as they were printed so pretty. Some soft prints and others more bold. I really remember the dress granny made for me was a bright red print and it has white lace added to the front to make it look like an apron. I was so proud of it, it became my Sunday best. Granny taught us so many things to make our lives easier especially she didn't want us to suffer the experience of having no father in the house. They made us take notice of what was expected from us, but at the same time she taught us to except the chores just as it would be in any household. It was all done with the firm hand of love. When we got on grannies nerves, doing all of the things kids get into trouble for, fighting, yelling and breaking things, granny would round us up and tell us she was going to straighten us up. Saying now sister go out and pick me a switch, you had better get a good one because if you don't you would not want me to go and get one. I guess I was a sleep walker and there were many nights that granny followed me to the neighbours, I would try to get in and then turn around and go home and back to bed. She said you were never to wake a sleep walker. Grandpa had two lots and one was devoted entirely for growing food for the winter, granny taught us to can our vegetables from the garden and the fruit from the trees. Walnuts from the tree was hulled and baked in the oven and sealed in jars for baking in the winter months. Being the younger of the two girls I always had the job of washing the jars under the China Berry Tree. The jars were so dirty after staying in the wash house for months after being used and put away. My hands were the smallest so I had to stick the rag along with my hand to clean the jars. Granny always calling from the house Sister do you have any ready for me? It seems that I was always rushed to do my job. Uncle Billy and Uncle Jack raised pigs for the FFA in high school as projects. I can still hear granny calling did you boys slop the hogs? The bucket is full by the porch. We also had chickens and it was the job of the little ones, Charles and I to gather the eggs. The big old rooster was not friendly every morning. Yes we also had bees for honey, I don't think there was much left to go to the store for. We had no refrigerator, just and old ice box. The ice man came once a week delivering ice. That was a treat as he would drive off we got to eat ice shavings, another smell from that era, was the smell of the wet burlap wrapped around the ice. I guess we were some of the most affluent families in the area. I had a friend that lived down the street in a tent with dirt floors and had no shoes to wear to school. I used to hide my shoes and go to school barefooted so she would not be the only one. Grandma Baker saw me hide my shoes at the bus stop she called my grandmother and told her what I had done. When I got off the bus the shoes were gone and I couldn't go home without shoes. Going through the door granny said where are your shoes? I told her I lost them," now tell me what happened to your shoes" she asked as she pulled them out and put them on the floor. Your mama worked hard to buy you those shoes and I had better not hear of this happening again. As usual she had all of the sayings that made sense to me such as "if you start a project finish it the best that you can, you never leave it unfinished, it may not be the best that's ever been done but it needs to be the best that you can do. Another was "if at first you don't succeed keep a sucking until you do succeed." Also "if you don't stick your foot out you can't get it chopped off" If nothings ventured it's nothing gained. At the same time she informed us that people were all the same except some had different color of skin. When we were real small about 2 yrs. old granny was sick and mama was about to give birth to Charles, things were bad and there was no money, a friend of the family whom happened to be black was raising a garden and he fed mama and us kids keeping us going through the winter. Another time when mama was nursing Charles the hospital told mama that a black baby was going to die as he was so allergic to cow's milk and he needed human milk. Mama nursed Charles and then nursed the black baby. I grew up with the saying pretty is as pretty does, and you reap what you sow, I actually came from a family of love. I was taught that you don't really need to have the things that are of no use to your way of life. You only need enough money to sustain your family and yourself, enough to furnish clothing food and shelter.

Uncle Billy

Living with my grandparents gave meaning to my life, a since of family and stability. My two Uncles, Billy (William Walter) and Jack (James Andrew) were like older brothers to me. They took over my care while Mary and granny went to work. To get us to make their beds they would leave a dime or quarter in the sheets, we had so much fun looking for the treasures that were left for us.

Uncle Billy whom we called "uncle peewee" was the favored one, he was the one who greeted us as we came home from school, gave us our first doll. He also had his way of punishing us, when we were bad and didn't do our share of the chores. He would hide us under the bed or behind furniture and not let us come out until he said so. We tried things as claiming to be thirsty and he put water to us in a can. One time while Uncle Billy was in the service, we got into his treasure of records and heated them to make pots, when they were hot you could mold the record into pretty petals for pots to hold plants they came with their own holes for drains and you could paint them many different colors. Until the day we lost Uncle Billy at the age of 76, he never forgave us for ruining his Jimmy Dorsey favorite. He never replaced his Glen Miller favorite. Every time I saw him and it was mentioned he got red in the face and said I came close to committing my first murder. I was really glad that he mellowed some in his old age. While Uncle Billy was in high school he broke the track record. It was the year of 1947 and it still stands today. I can believe that story myself as you can see from the picture he was not a very big fellow. He said he was 5'6" and weighed in at 138 lbs. When the holidays came around he was always there to see that we had the best Christmas ever. When I graduated from the 8th grade he gave me my 1st watch it was in a gold color and was a Bolivia. Talk about a man that could spoil a child. As I entered High School he went into the army and later the National Guard. While he was in the service he married his sweetheart, only to have her leave him for another lover. This happened only after three days of marriage. Her name was Sadie, she stayed married to her husband all of the years of Uncle Billy's life having three children. Uncle Billy would never give her a divorce so all of her kids had his last name. After he married Aunt Ada he divorced her. He later met and married an older woman she didn't fit into the family very well. You know the type they always want you to wait on them. In his later years he met the woman of his dreams and ours. It was such a delight to finely see him so happy. Aunt Ada brought so much company and joy to his life.

    Uncle Jack used to take us on his dates with his girlfriend Lora Bickerstaff to Hart Park in Bakersfield a lot. Later it would be long drives to the mountains and picked wild flowers. The hills would just be aflame with so much color, orange poppies, blue lupines and Indian paintbrushes. They were so solid you couldn't move without crushing them. Some of the most colorful Easters were when we would go to the hills in Arvin and hunt Easter eggs then take long walks listening to Uncle Jack tell us stories. They always ended with him telling us that he loved us. Another time

James Andrew (Jack)

we went to Hart Park for swimming and a game of Base Ball. They had a train in the park that took you all around also a merry go round. After Uncle Jack and Aunt Lora were married they tried so hard to have a family. Aunt Lora had so much trouble with conception that she underwent surgery to be able to get pregnant, it still never happened. One of Aunt Lora's sisters, who had children of her own, had the opportunity of adopting a set of twin boys. Aunt Lora pleaded to her sister to let her and Uncle Jack adopt the boys as they already had a family of two girls. It happened they got the twins Ronald and Donald Searcy it made their life complete. They were finally a happy family. But wait Aunt Lora was sick all the time, they soon found out she was expecting a child of her own. The twins never knew what happened to make their lives change so much. After Gordon Dale was born there was no love left for the twins. At this time of his life Uncle Jack became violent towards a lot of people; I never knew what it was to make him change. He always carried a knife or gun and when he had a confrontation with someone it was always violent with him drawing his knife to hurt someone. As the twins got older, about 15 Uncle Jack threw them out of the house disowning them. I felt so sorry for them. They had no place to go, so different friends of theirs, families took them in and saw to it to get them through high school. They really were good kids. Donnie turned to drinking and Ronnie went into the Navy. In the Navy he studied electricity, when he was discharged he made his living in the electrical field. Today they are both happy and Donnie finally got on the right track and he builds special projects for his customers.

Uncle Billy

Living with my grandparents and uncles to take care of us gave mama time to work and bring her share of the income to the house hold. This also gave her plenty of time for dating. While our daddy was in the war mama worked as a dance partner at the USO on the base. I assume this is where she met plenty of her suitors. It seemed like there was a long line of uncles, if you get my drift. I guess I was told to call them uncle. Around 1946 mama worked as a bar maid at the local bowling alley. She worked long and hard hours, saving all of her tips in a jar on the bar, one night some on stole the money from her jar and she was really upset as she was saving to buy her children coats for Christmas. There was this young fellow that had his eyes on her and he liked her so much that he took her to buy coats for us. This gesture placed him right into her heart. So much kindness for children he had never met. His name was Bill Shultz a member of a long time farming family. As Bill dated mama he usually included us on the rides to the beach, mountains and this man loved to fish so there were a lot of fishing trips. I remember one day asking him "Are you going to be my new daddy" he replied it sounds like a good idea. There were not many pictures taken of Bill and Mary, only the wedding picture and shower pictures.

STARTING OUR NEW LIFE AS A NEW FAMILY

THIS IS THE BEGINNING of our new life. With this marriage I got two new sisters, Beverly and Judy Shultz. Judy was 7 days older than Ruby and Beverly was 3 months older than I and we were 22 months older than Charles. We became a family of five that day. Mama and Daddy went to Reno to get married, Ted and Margie was their witnesses. Beverly and Judy knew nothing of the marriage until mom and dad picked them up in Oregon, where they were staying with Aunt Lena and Uncle Gene, dad's sister. Beverly claims that daddy walked in and said this is your new mother and you are to love her as your own. At this point Beverly decided that she didn't like me as I was stealing her share of her daddy's love. I didn't understand this as I was so in awe of having more sisters and a new father. When they married I was in the 3rd grade, Bev was put in my class so that I could show her my friends and help her to make friends with them. She wanted nothing to do with them, nor me, it never crossed my mind that she had a bad case of jealousy. Daddy was a farmer and this was a new way of life for me, at eight yrs. of age I had to go to the fields with daddy to work. No, farm labor was not new to me, but now I have to actually go and work in the fields myself.

Before mom and daddy married mama got sick and couldn't keep any food down she went to the hospital and had to have a hysterectomy, as you know it left her barren. Daddy led her to believe, it didn't make a difference to him that she could no longer bear children. Unknown to mama daddy had always wanted a son OF HIS OWN. Not another man's child, there for he could never give Charles the love he needed to become a man of substance. He always ignored him and focused on us. Mama and daddy set the rules when they first got married as to how they would go about taking care of correction problems. Not allowing us to work them against each other, if mom corrected Judy or Beverly and they ran to tell daddy that mama punished them, then they would get it just as hard, or worse than mama had dished up. It went the same way with him doing the correction. We soon learned that it didn't pay to back talk, I remember saying" but you said I could" and felt the sting of being hit in the mouth with mama's hand. What did you say, then I said" but you said" and again I felt the sting of the hand, it did not take me long to learn to keep my mouth shut. Another thing was who did this? No one answers and it's asked again. Ok I will get the belt and get all of you then I will know that I got the guilty one. At this point it usually made the guilty one come forward, sometimes it didn't because we never would rat on each other, especially if it was Charles, his punishment would be something that none of us could bear.

When mama and daddy got home and came home to the house on the farm. Another four room house only this one you entered through the kitchen went to the living room, into mama and daddy's room then into the room five children would share. It had two sets of bunk beds and Charles had a roll away bed. We each had a shelf in this big cabinet and Charles's stuff went into a box under his bed. We were all excited to be together as a family. Daddy never did adopt us as he claimed it was too expensive and we girls would be changing our names as adults. The house had only cold running water you had to heat water outside in a huge black iron pot. You had to use wood to heat it. We used a number 4 wash tub to bathe in, in the middle of the kitchen floor, once a week you got to be first and have hot water you always hated it when you were last. They kept us on a tight schedule we were always in bed by 8'clock. Every evening daddy would say ok it's time to drain your lilies and lizard and head for bed.

Again mama got sick, it was nothing to hear the ambulance pull up to the house and they would be giving mama oxygen because she couldn't breathe. Eventually she was hospitalized and had an ingrown goiter removed. Mama's health made daddy start a routine that lasted until we all got married off as adults. Two of the girls would stay home and do all of the house chores and the other two went to the fields with daddy and Charles. The girls would switch off every week, Charles never got a break. Daddy had 360 acres of land in Wasco and no help on the farm but the kids of the family walla!!! As we became teen agers we wanted to be paid for our work so that we could start paying for our own things, like clothes and such. Daddy replied you are part of this family so you work the same as I do.

Some of the chores included feeding the chickens, gathering the eggs, and all of the house work, including the laundry. Keep in mind we were only 8 or 9 years old while all of this was thrust upon us. Talk about children growing up fast. Oh yes we had to prepare all the meals and pack lunches for the rest of the family that went to work the fields. Daddy showed us how to measure the raw products and read recipes, we were on our own. Daddy never complained about how things were done, I guess we did fine for our age. To do the laundry we had to heat water in the big black pot and the washing machine was outside so we did not have to carry the hot water to far to load the washer. The washer had the washing tub for the hot water and detergent; we pulled the number 4 wash tub that was on wheels to the other side, there were two tubs one for the 1st rinse and one for the 2nd rinse. The machine was electric. It had a wringer on top we had to run the clothes though the wringer from tub to tub. Once when it was mine and Beverly's turn to do laundry everything was going fine until I got my arm caught in the wringer instead of Beverly hitting the release button she ran my hand and arm back through. It could have broken my arm but no harm done. It was sore for a week or so, still it didn't get me out of my chores.

Judy and I had to do the dishes one night, we got it done very quickly, daddy thought it was really too quick. He asked did you finish the dishes already, we answered yes daddy, did you put them away, yes daddy. I'll be in a minute to check them. Right then and there we knew we were had. We had not done the dishes we just put them in the cupboards. When daddy found them we got the spanking of our lives for lying and had to wash every dish and pot in the kitchen we also had to do the dishes for a week straight, instead of getting to trade off. Now tell me how he was not going to notice the dirty dishes in the cupboards.

We raised chickens and turkeys for the general public. We worked every Thanksgiving and Christmas butchering our chickens and turkeys for customers that had placed orders for the holidays. I remember trying to kill a chicken and nearly chopped off my toe. I still have the scar today. When we would go to gather eggs and feed the chickens there was one rooster that didn't like Judy. Every day when she went outside that rooster would chase her around the yard holding onto the seat of her pants. Our chickens were allowed to roam the yard sometimes while we were cleaning the pen it was not safe for Judy. When we were not doing chores we played outside. One of our favorite games was Evie, Ivey, Over. This was a game that you threw the ball over the house to the kids on the other side they in turn returned the ball calling Evie, Ivey Over. You never knew where the ball would land. In the house we played jacks in the floor and pickup sticks at the table Grandpa had taught us checkers and dominos. Remember in our day there was no television. One of the things the girls liked doing was singing together while we did dishes after dinner. Mama even joined in. The only one left out of the singing was me Dorothy they all knew the music teacher said I couldn't carry a tune even if it was in a bucket.

I think one of the events that will never be forgotten was the outhouse. It was a two holler, one time Charles was in the outhouse and he took the puppies along. As you have guessed one of them fell into the toilet. Charles went running into the house to tell mama about the drama. Daddy whipped Charles all the way back to the outhouse; he turned over the outhouse and lowered Charles down to pick up the puppy needless to say he never took the puppies with him again.

One of our favorite things to play was to play house. We spent hours making our walls out of dirt. We used brooms to sweep up enough dirt to make a line that would define the rooms in our house and we used card board boxes for our furniture. On a Sunday we spent the whole day living our lives in our dirt home and cardboard furniture. We would get sick and one of us would get the Dr. and make us all well again. Being poor never gave us an excuse not to use our imaginations and create things to entertain ourselves. One day mama and daddy brought home bikes for us to share, our first new toys. Charles got a boys bike it was his alone. We girls had to share the girl's bike, learning to tell time became very important at this time, you were given 15 minutes for your turn and you had better not go over or all hell was to be paid.

We worked in the grapes also. Daddy had about 25 acres of grapes on the home place, in the winter he started pruning them and we followed wrapping and tying the vines. This was done in the month of November when the fog was thick and it was cold and dripping wet, the vines you had just wrapped came flying loose and hit you in the face. Oh how I hated this job, I don't like to be cold. When it came to harvest time we helped the crew cut grapes, making trays and laying them on the ground to dry. Daddy's grapes were used to make raisins. After a few weeks drying time it was time to roll the trays, this was a job that had to be done fast and to beat the rains. The rains would cause the raisins to mildew and he could lose the whole crop. This was devastating as you had all of your money in the crop and weather could make you lose everything. You only made one crop a year and it was a long day waiting for the next one to roll around. A few times he got caught in the rains and had to spend even more money trying to sort the moldy ones from the good ones, another expense in an already devastating venture. He must do it to try to get enough money out of the crop to pay the loan back and get financing for the following season. Not much left to take care of the family. This is one of the reasons a farmer has to plant more than one type of crop, this allowed for money behind different crops and just a few more pay days per year for the farmer. Daddy worked out a financing agreement with SA Camp for money to keep his family going at the rate of $500.00 per mo. Then Camp would put up the money for the following years crops. At this rate we never had much, but we did have enough.

During grape harvest we would cut raisins for a neighboring farmer and earn enough money to buy material to make our school clothes. We had one sewing machine between the four girls to make our clothes. Did I mention it was only two weeks until the school year would start? We only had enough time to make one outfit each. Off to school; for another year, books and binders all in tow. So much to do and so little time must learn to share.

Daddy had to sell the home place to give his sisters their share of the property's worth after Grandpa Shultz passed away. This left him with the 360 acres on the other side of Wasco. He wanted to build us a better home. I remember daddy and mama discussing the probability of building on the ranch. Daddy thought that there were just too many mosquitoes and it could make us all sick being bitten too much. Mom and dad decided on a lot in the town of Shafter and then he hired Jim Dandy to build our home. Can you imagine building a three bedroom house for $15,000.00? To us it was a castle. My first bath in a bath tub in a tiled bathroom, such luxury, this was in 1952. Now my life was taking another turn in the economic world. Our new home had three bedrooms, one for mom and dad one for Judy and Ruby and one for Beverly and I to share. They never let us room as we wanted it was always as they said. It had a large living room and dining room together with a door out back. Kitchen and service porch and half bath with shower, off of the kitchen there was a den that was made into Charles's room. He finally had his own space. What a wonderful thing for him.

In this time I was in the 7th grade and we started having art in school. We played with clay and made different things, our teacher was Mrs. McClure, she taught us so many things like working the clay to get all of the air bubbles out and we could pick a project to work on. Most of the kids made ash trays for their parents, I had to be different. I molded my clay into a lady carrying a bible. I Thought I did a good job on it and I guess my mother did to. She kept it all of those years in the display case in the dining room and now I have it in my home, it's at least 60 yrs old. In the eighth grade we did painting and working with building maps using homemade clay out of salt, water, flour and paper. We could build mountains and valleys. After they were dry we painted them making the Painted Desert and beautiful mountains.

It was announced that there would be an art show-contest. I was so thrilled with my abilities using paints and clay that Mrs. McClure said that I should enter and see what I could do. I did just that, I painted a tree that was shedding its leaves, and it had a road along the houses on it. Oh my god I took 1st place. This gave me the bug to forge ahead into the art world.

Our father had his own way of helping us to cope with the realism of life as it is dealt to us. When the 1st girl started her period she thought she was dying and came running to mom and told her she was bleeding to death. Mom is the emotional one so she was of no help. Daddy said, come here honey and he explained to her the process of the female body preparing its self for women hood. He explained about the egg and ovaries and the fertilization of the egg and how a baby forms from this process. This sounds as though it's something we should have known at this age she was only 9yrs old. Well daddy did as he always did and said I will only tell you once so you had better listen up and pay attention. He then proceeded to make us each wear a towel so we knew how our sister felt.

As you know the two older girls were a year ahead of us in school so when they were old enough to date daddy sat us all on the couch and explained about dating. We had to have the boy come and meet our parents before any permission was ever given. He set a curfew and it had better never be broken or we would be staying home for a full six weeks and with no phone. There was no TV or Cell Phones or Computers so he didn't have to monitor those items. He then proceeded to tell us what boys would try to pull on dates and he would show us at the same time. He explained what was permissible and what we could not let them do. He ended the lecture saying now if you get yourselves pregnant, don't think you are going to go and give away one of my grandchildren you will stay right here and have it. There will be no adoption in this family. In the 1950's it was scornful to be pregnant out of wedlock. He finished I know these boys will try these things because it hasn't been that long since I was a young whippersnapper myself. By the time I started High School and dating I thought if a guy didn't try those things explained by my father, there must be something wrong with guy and he was left by the wayside.

Life just kept continuing as usual chopping cotton, going to the beach, and fishing at Lake Isabella. One day Aunt Naomi and Uncle Otto came out to the ranch and wanted us to go have a picnic and play in the water on the Kern River that ran through Bakersfield. Daddy said ok but he had to have all of the cotton rows weeded between, point A and point B, so that it could be cultivated for his next set of water. My cousins Bernice, Maxine and Jerry Searcy all pitched in and helped to get the chore done. It was wonderful by the river and playing in the water with my cousins. Daddy and Uncle Otto were the best of buddies and they both always included the whole family in their fishing plans and it was usually a place on the river or Lake Isabella, best of all the beach and deep sea fishing. Charles so loved his fishing, I guess this was the one way that daddy and Charles connected. Hunting was also a big thing for daddy all of his buddies and son-in laws would gather for the dove and pheasant hunting and the women and kids gathered at the house to have meals ready for them when they would come in. Aunt Naomi and Uncle Otto were the first ones to get this new machine called Television. It was wonderful this cause the families to spend even more time together. Every Thursday night we would go to their house and watch the fights. All TV at this time was a little round screen in a big case. On yes only in black and white. When the adults were watching the screen the kids were off playing house or hospital and Dr. It was a great life. We spent so much time together that you would have thought we were all one family.

Let's get back to the main meat of this life's story. When the house was built I was only in the 7th grade making me about 11 years old, can you see me sitting on that couch listening about what the boys could do and would try to do. By the time it was for me to date it was all old hat. Any way when I started High School at Shafter High I wanted to take art. When you were in high school you could have electives to start you on your journey in life. This was when I was hit with the bomb shell, no you can't take art. Some day if you can't find a husband to take care of you, you must be able to take care of yourself. Therefore being a secretary is a good line of work and you could live on the wages. Art will not support you, so I had to do as I was told. I then armed myself with the business classes that were available, shorthand, typing, and bookkeeping, you know all of the boring stuff it was not art. I soon forgot about being an artist and just living day to day doing my share of the chores and just looking for the day that I could graduate and leave home.

Ruby was the one who gave mom and dad all the trouble. She fell madly in love with a boy named Gary Bromwell. His parents thought Ruby was not good enough for their son and mom and dad felt the same way about Gary. Gary stole his mom and dad's car and they ran away to get married they were caught in Yuma Arizona. They were forbidden to see each other, then one night daddy caught them in the back yard making love and he nearly beat Ruby to death, the Dr. said one more blow would have killed her. Gary went on and joined the service and was killed in a jeep accident. Ruby was sent to live with Willard our father. Ruby was so beautiful that she could have any one of the guys at school. That long flowing blond hair and blue eyes, her skin tanned so easily and was a gorgeous color of tan. Ruby always had her way with mom, she was mom's favorite child and it seemed she could do no wrong in mom's eyes. If I sound envious I am I would have loved to be treated in that way. At one time during high school Ruby was staying with Aunt Lena and Uncle Gene going to school there, she got active in drama and had the lead part in Little Abner playing Daisy Mae.

Even as a small child granny would treat us different, granny saying that grandma Sanders always favored her little dark haired kitten. I was so small that I can't remember any warmth from that family while we were still a family.

Mom and dad became heavy drinkers and they were drunk or in some stage of it every day and night. We had parties at our house for our high school friends and almost all the time every one came. We were very popular, we were the only ones who had parents stay at the party and furnish the booze. Mama loved dancing with the young boys and dad was busy mixing the drinks. One time when Uncle Billy came home on leave he found out about my drinking and decided he was going to put a stop to it. He got me so drunk, beer, wine, vodka, gin, and brandy all in the same evening. I was so drunk that I couldn't lie down on the bed because it was spinning so fast. The next day I had to go to work in the cotton fields in Wasco. It was so hot and the rows were a quarter mile long, by the time I got to the far end I was vomiting so severely, but I had to turn around and go back to the other end. Here we had a ditch with water running for irrigation I would just plop into the ditch to the waist and drink water, turn around and do it again. Needless to say I have never taken another drink like that night. I can't stand the aroma of whiskey without getting sick to this day. Judy was also a defiant one she was going to do want she wanted to do. Judy ran away with her bow Ronald Scoggins to Modesto they got married and lived with his mother for awhile. We all loved Ronnie he was one of us. Judy was another beauty, she had a head of hair to die for and it was naturally curly. Both she and Ruby were tall and slender and had pretty much the same personalities. Judy and Ron had three children Joe, Janice and Karla. Their marriage did not last for very many years. Judy raised her family alone being a waitress; with her personality she would make very good tips. Between husbands Judy moved to Bakersfield, I became her care taker, helping to find her an apartment and she found a job. Did I say Judy was quite a drinker? Well she drank quite heavily, one night she left her apartment and went downstairs down the street to a pay phone called the police to come and pick her up, they obliged. The next day I had to pick her up from the jail, I saw one of our workers there, he says Mrs. Slikker what are you doing here? I asked him the same question, picking up my brother and I said I'm after my sister. We had a good laugh. She then met and married a man by the name of Wilson, he beat her all the time and she was deathly afraid of him. One time she called me to pick her up, she would be hiding in the garbage dumpster behind her apartment, I got there and called her name and she came crawling out and I took her home with me. Later in her years she married two more times. Her last one led her to be in New Mexico around the same area as Ruby. They at this time became very close to each other. Ruby playing the mother hen especially after Judy's husband died of Cancer. One day, as Judy was in so much pain all the time with her arthritis, Judy took some of her husband's pain medication and it overdosed her as she was already taking a medication by injection for the pain.

We never got to go to the Senior Prom at high school daddy said he could not afford a dress for each of us to wear for one night so nobody should go. It was all fine and good he had a reason for the decision.

Let's take Charles he was always the one left in left field you might say, I have told you that he and dad didn't get along that well. Charles stole money from mama's purse and ran away of course he was caught and brought back home. Living with four girls running around in various stages of dress didn't help a fellow from thinking all kinds of things. Charles went to a pay phone and made an obscene phone call to one of our neighbors she recognized his voice and had her husband call the police. They caught him in the phone booth with her still on the line. He was sent to juvenile for two weeks, when he was released he didn't want to come home to a house full of girls. He loved being with the fellows it seemed like camp to him. After he was home about two weeks he stole money again from mom and this time he made it to Willard. Willard's wife was jealous of all of us so she made Willard put him in the Orphanage they called mom in California and she went and picked him up. When it happened again this time Willard signed him into the Army at the age of 17. Being with all of these older men and having wild weekend furloughs did not help what he thought sex was about. The love and tenderness that is associated with true love and giving your body and soul to another. While Charles was in the army he played in the army band and later he was sent to Viet Nam with the 101st Air Born Division. While he was there he worked as a demolition leader setting bombs and such. Charles told me horror stories about serving in the Viet Nam war, he and his partner was setting bombs or mines as they were called. After the job was completed he was sent to town for more supplies, while he was away an order came to dismantle the mines since he was in town his partner started without him, he set one off accidently and was killed. This gave Charles night mares clear up until his own death at the age of 64. One day I noticed that he had false teeth, I asked what happened you always had the prettiest teeth in the family it was the butt end of a rifle, while I was point man on patrol; the enemy butted him so to be silent and surprise the squad. When he came to in the hospital he had no teeth and his jaw was broken. He also talked about how they were treated by our own people up on their return. How would you like having your life on the line all the time and come home just to be called murderers and have human shit thrown in your face. While in Viet Nam he was sprayed with Agent Orange and later in life that was what he died from was the cancer it caused in the lungs. As Charles grew older he was celebrating his 27th birthday, someone in the crowd slipped a drug in his drink. When he came to he had kidnapped a young girl and had a knife held to her throat. He took her back home and was arrested. I went to the jail and asked him Charles did you really do this? His answer was yes so go away and let them do with me what they want to. All I could think of what can I do it will ruin my business when it is found out that my brother had kidnapped a young girl not thinking about what was happening at the time I was thinking me me me. Later I realized that our names were different now and we would not be associated as family. When he went to trial they found him unsound to face the charges and court. He was sent to the Atascadero Mental hospital for four years. Now they wanted to try him again. I called my friend that was a criminal attorney and he said for $500.00 he would see what he could do. Later that same day the attorney called and said he could be released that day and he wanted a pack of cigarettes. He had lost everything his family and any self respect that he ever had. He later married his probation officers sister Mary and they had two boys they moved and lived their life in Visalia Ca. Charles and Mary had two sons Charlie Jr. and Tony. Charles wanted his boys to be the big tough boys and be able to take on anyone; he gave them Karate lessons and worked hard to toughen them up. He was so proud when they graduated from high school. I don't think Charles graduated so this was a big deal to him. Charlie never followed through with his dad's desires he became a nurse and worked in the hospital in Visalia, Tony now was so completely different he looked so tough you would be afraid of him only he had the tenderness of heart to all around him. He got work as a security guard. Charlie also came out of the closet and let the world know he was gay. This was hard for Charles to accept, but accept he did and continued his moral support in the lives of both.

It just seems to be everything I did Charles would want to do. He divorced Mary and moved over to the beach just as I had. He asked to stay for a few days and then called a friend and went to have dinner with her, he never returned. He moved into her home and a few months later he married Maxine. He and Maxine had a wonderful relationship, she had a boat and Charles fished with her son all the time. Maxine even fished a lot. It seemed that he had found his real soul mate and I was so happy for him.

There was a time in high school that Bev and I were in band and it was football season. The band has to always play at the half time performance if you did not show up it was an automatic F on your report card. In our family you could not go anywhere without permission. We came home from school to ask permission and we had to be back at school within the hour to catch the band bus, no mom or dad. We talked it over and left a note for them and let them know where we were. The game was at Garces High School in Bakersfield, we knew we were in deep trouble. Remember the rule six weeks. We got the whole time with no excuses accepted.

There were many days that were fun on the ranch when daddy was in a good mood. We used to play in the reservoir making trails through the tulles' so that daddy could go froging. He always claimed that frog legs tasted like chicken. Daddy also liked to try to get us to taste snake that was going too far. He taught us how to shoot the shot gun. We used to ride on the fenders and point out the rabbits yes we had cotton tail quite often. One time while the cotton was small and we were chopping it mama was helping that day, she started screaming and flying out of her pants it was so funny, a lizard had ran up her pant leg and she thought it was a snake. There were a lot of rattle snakes on the ranch. It was nothing to get there in the morning and see them wrapped around the wheel of the tractor. I learned how to drive tractor before I was old enough to drive. One day daddy was going to check water, he got out of the pickup and said pick me up on the other end. WHAT!!! I had never driven what a way to learn. By the way the pickup was moving when he got out. Just ahead there was an embankment I just knew that if I hit it I would crash, daddy laughed at me as I panicked as I hit the embankment and the car just travelled on up onto the dirt road, boy did I have a lot to learn. Daddy always grew hay; it had to be cut raked and rolled for the drying process. When a big whirl wind would come up, I used to say how I loved the smell of fresh cut alfalfa, daddy would say since you love the smell of fresh alfalfa take the pitch fork and shuck the hay meaning putting it back in the line. One season daddy gave us each a check of hay to plant and take care of. We could keep the money it made less the cost of growing. Daddy hooked the float to the tractor, explaining to me to look back every once in awhile to make sure everything was still in good order. Daddy rode on the float so he could broadcast the seed, I drove all the way to the other end and when I got the tractor turned around I had no float or dad, they were in the middle of the field. Uh ho this is what he meant to look behind for.

We had hogs and had to chase them from one corner of the ranch to the other. We raised milo for pig feed and field corn. The milo (sorghum) was cut by hand with a curved knife and thrown into a half trailer. We harvested five acres this way me, Charles, me and my sisters. The field corn was a horse of another color. The leaves were so dry and they would cut your hands and face. I sometimes thought he planned all of this stuff for us to do to keep us out of trouble and it worked. The sow was named Rosy and the boar was Sam. They produced many piglets that were sold for profits, one day Sam charged daddy he got the gun and ended the charge. Sam was so large that the neighboring farmers stopped and helped daddy and us kids to load him in the pickup. He was taken home to butcher. Uncle Jack came to help hoist the pig up on the swing set so that daddy could gut him in that position, while he was busy Uncle Jack cut off the tail. Daddy screamed what the hell did you do that for? The tail could be used to turn and roll the hog while we are scraping the fur from the hide. It was finally successful. We cooked the skin and fat to make cracklings' and render the fat to lard. The feet were pickled and the head was used to make minced meat. Nothing ever went to waste.

In 1952 we had a large earth quake in Bakersfield, Shafter and the surrounding towns. It toppled the clock tower in downtown Bakersfield. Daddy came screaming, what the hell they are bombing us. The roar was so loud and all of the transformers were blowing up. Then complete silence, we all gathered outside and saw the neighbors doing the same. It was so soon after World War 11 that is what made daddy think we were being bombed, he had lost his brother Uncle Harry in that war just after it was declared over. One of the things the earth quake caused was the sanding up of the irrigation well and daddy had planted potatoes that year. They were ready to be harvested and baked in the ground instead. Sometimes I think if daddy had any luck it was no luck at all.

As we grew older and our older sisters were gone on their life's venture and Charles was no longer home Beverly and I got along a little better. We were actually cordial to each other yet we never shared friends or activities. Finally it was 1958 and we were graduating from High School. We were getting ready for the next chapter in our lives. Beverly always wanted to be a beautician so she enrolled in Beauty College. I went on to Bakersfield College. We came home one day and there was a different car in the drive way. We ran into the house to see who was visiting and daddy said how do you girls like your new car for driving to school? It was a beautiful 1949 Chevy Convertible. We drove it for the next two years. Beverly got married in the 1st year and the car became mine.

Through the high school years I guess you might say that there was a lot of competition between us. Bev always helped her friends with homework and sometimes doing it for them. She was smart and studious. I was no dummy either but I liked to do things like push my deadlines for homework completion. If a project was to take a month to complete it she would take the month and do all the things necessary to make a perfect project. Take the interior decorating class a month to find paint samples, flooring ect. She took all the time needed, Bev got a B grade. Me I took all of one week through my project together and made an A for the project. Needles to say it didn't help the relationship. Bev had been friends for a long time with Johnny Sivils, they soon fell in love and started going steady. Bev and Johnny got married and Bev completed her Beauty School they left Bakersfield and moved to San Jose, here they started their family and John got a job at IBM he had his own office things were going smooth and all of a sudden he was out of work. John and Bev moved to a smaller community, they purchased an office supply store. John was home a lot and watched the kids while Bev ran the store. This works for some people, somewhere along the line Bev took painting lessons; she is the one who inspired me a lot. When she came home and came to my dress shop she also gave me one of her paintings. Today she still wants it back. Bev and John had three children one boy and two girls. Christopher, Patty and Julie all are wonderful kids.

Remember how I stated I hated farm work? Well I also said I will never marry a farmer as I don't want to do this type of work for the rest. Now look what God sent me to love another damn farmer. He was just beautiful I couldn't keep from falling in love and I still am. It's been 57years this year. Love this man.

I had gone on to Bakersfield College and decided it was so different from what I thought it would be, I could actually pick and choose my own destiny in this school. Mom and Dad had lifted their hold on me so I actually felt like a whole person. Still Art did not cross my mind. I was so entrenched in Business. I chose to take child development courses and nutrition classes, involving chemistry, sewing and modeling classes. Ultimately I joined the Hepsilon Club. In high school I was in the Band and marched with them for four years, now I joined the Gaydetts, the flag twirlers that marched behind the band in parades and football games. Long story short the Hepsilon Club and the Ag Club got together to build a home coming float for the biggest game of the year. Being a farmer's daughter I pulled a trailer to the house where we were going to be working on it. A young farmer had also pulled a trailer his was bigger so they chose his for the parade. I talked to him and my best friend Carol liked him also, she got him to take her home that night. The next day she said I'll never go with another boy you pick out, I asked why, she said all he did was ask about you. A smile went across my heart. As we got close to finishing the float, John said to get my attention; I bet my horn is louder than your horn.

He had a 1957 Chevy Bell air Two Door Hardtop. I said I don't think so let's try them, I blew my horn which was loud and then he blew his. The noise was astounding as he had mounted a truck horn to his car. Cute!! I had two very cute friends that helped on the float and one I knew John had a crush on (we had never had a date) he came to me and asked do you care if Lacretia Duggan and Betty Wooley ride with me in the parade? I looked him in the eye and said no, but if you do don't ever ask me for a date. That evening he pulled the float alone and after the half time came up where I was and asked would you like to get something to eat after the game? I answered yes and we started going steady on our first date. We got married on our Easter Break on April 9th 1960 and graduated that same year. Now was the time to get my trailer back to Uncle Johnnies house, John told his ag teacher that he would take it to Shafter but that girl had to come to. This pleased me to no end. The Ag Club had parties and the Home ex. Club had parties. One time when we were at the Ag Club party I was sitting on the ice cream maker and Johns' friends were laughing and having a good time and I guess I was too. This made John so mad that he took me home and just dropped me off. This was one of the times my parents were so afraid that I was going to lose him. Daddy wanted him to be part of our family. I was told by my parents to straighten myself up and fly right or he won't be back. I don't care was my reply.

COLLAGE YEARS

To TELL THE TRUTH I really didn't want to go to college, but if I didn't I would be stuck in the fields with no way to have a life of my own, when we me, Beverly, and Cathy went to enroll we got off of the city bus to early and had to walk for about four miles to the college, on the way we came across a Marine recruiting office and just marched inside to try to enroll. We were all about the same age only 17yrs old, not old enough to enlist without parents signature, we all passed with flying colors. The Marines notified our parents and daddy said "give college" one year if you still want to enlist he would sign the papers. But during my first year I met the rest of my life in the form of a tall farm boy named John. Nothing could take the place of this farmer in my heart. The rest of the college time was getting to know John and waiting for us to be old enough to marry and make our lives move forward. During our dating years the drive in was the big thing a lot of loving going on in those cars. The Everly Brothers had a song out that year Wake up Little Susie. John and I had a date going up on the river, he loved his fishing too, came back went to dinner and then the movies. We fell asleep and didn't wake up until about three in the morning, no cars left on the movie lot, we felt lucky that they had a way for us to get out.

Next was explaining all this to my parents. Daddy so liked John that he took away my curfew. Some of the fights we would have I would storm around the house and daddy would say you had better straighten up or he won't come back. I answered with I don't care if he never comes back. I guess love can weather almost any storm.

April 9th Easter Vacation wedding bells and honeymoon. What a way to spend Easter Break. The few nights before our wedding we were looking for a motel to spend our wedding night. John rear ended another car at the Drive Inn it happened to be a friend of his. John had to call his dad and we used his car for John to take me home. Johns' car was being fixed fast so that it would be drivable for the honeymoon the next day. Ok next is the wedding we got married in the Baptist Church in Wasco on 4th St. Rev. Krug performed the ceremony. I am now Mrs. John William Slikker Jr. and I was determined to love, honor and cherish him forever. I felt that we had a good foundation to build a marriage on both coming from farming families and I had been through it all. I learned to cope when things were not turning out the way they should. I kept remembering my saying I will not marry a farmer, I will not have a damn farmer and I will not work in the fields all the rest of my life. Well now we all know how that turned out.

We found our first house a month or so before the wedding and spent our time at school and putting our new home together. John's Uncle Kampe gave us a chair and his mom gave us the most god awful couch, black with large brightly colored flowers on it. Our new castle, anyway I felt that way, was located on Quantico in Bakersfield, CA. It was not a long drive to school and John and I had some classes together, making the most of marriage, John dropped out of this class, math and Social Studies. I hated math so much especially thought problems, never could figure out if you added, subtracted or divided to get the answers. John was a wiz in math and refused to help me at all.

I had a job as the home Ec. Secretary and at a drive in, in Bakersfield. I also worked chopping cotton and doing farm chores. Still I carried 17 Units at school and carried a B average. After getting married I got to drop all of my jobs, finally I am off the farm. Living in a dream world with what I considered the best man in the world, I still do today after 57 years of marriage. I was once asked "how can you love and stay married for such a long time." Respect and love most of all you have to learn to play together and do things together, no girls' night out or boys' night out. Do things as a couple best of all be the best friends in the world. When your man likes to fish, go fishing, carry his string of fish and carry on a conversation about what he is doing, when you are doing a project he should also get involved in some way. As we continued on with school things were great. One morning as John was working outside in the flowers, I slept in upon waking I went in took a hot shower and proceeded to join John outside by the flowers I remember getting light headed and then passing out. What happened, what's wrong, when I came to I was in bed and John was scared to death. The next day I went to the Dr., he diagnosed me as to being pregnant. This was thrilling news for me as I wanted a little boy like his father. Jeans, t-shirt rolled up sleeves. Wonderful!! A few days later we met John's mom and dad for dinner, we gave them the wonderful news that they were becoming grandparents. John's mom started crying you cannot do this to me I am too young to be a grandmother. Come June 1960 we graduated the three of us. The school would not let me use my new name as I had gone to school always as Sanders. Bummer!!! While we were in our little nest the neighborhood was becoming violent, a neighbors' son kept fighting with her she was elderly, one time he shot at her. We decided to find a new place and move. No one would rent to us because of me being pregnant. Who wanted a young couple with a baby' tearing up their property. We even checked into buying a house of our own. John told his dad about our dilemma, he told us we could move into the little farm house down the dirt road and we will see about building a house for you and your new family. This house was built out of cement, the shower was awful. The rats ran all over the house at night, you could hear them running across the floor. When you would pull your car into the parking structure the rats ran everywhere. Grandpa Slikker gave us a couple of cats and it did not take long for them to clear them all up. At night you could hear them chasing the rats across the room and sliding into the wall creating a loud bang. There was no phone service at this house only a dirt road in; with the baby on the way what would we do if it rained? Oh yes we would park a tractor out by the house, just in case. We went to the Christmas parade, when we got home my water broke we headed down the dirt road going to his mothers' house to use the phone to call the Dr. for instructions. This was how the plan was supposed to work. This was the first time that I experienced the feeling of not being loved by John's family the way he was with mine. My grandpa even made the remark that he couldn't visit me in my home because I had married out of my class. Apparently this was how my new mother-in-law also felt. This house was about a mile down a dirt road and we had no phone, service was not available. We left and went to Johns' mom and dads' place to call the Dr. his mom said no just take her to the hospital. Four hours later I gave birth to our first son Jon Edwin Slikker.

John and I preceded picking out a floor plan and dad hired a builder to build the house, can you believe the contract was only one page. The house was the most beautiful building in the world to me it had a white stone roof and rock front. The kitchen had all of the latest modern appliances, built in refrigerator, micro wave built in oven and range, garbage disposal and best of all a dishwasher. I had three bedrooms and two baths. A living room with a white rock fireplace, all of a sudden I was uptown on the farm. All of this cost for the house was $21,000.00 what a beautiful place to raise our family.

As we lived our lives I became pregnant a second time, I was thrilled as maybe I would have my little girl this time around. My tummy kept getting bigger and the Dr. confirmed that I was pregnant and set an appointment for the following month, this visit he could not hear a heartbeat and told me to stay off of my feet and do as little as possible, aye with a small child to care for, I did the best I could. Each month I kept getting bigger and the Dr. would say he still couldn't hear the heart beat. This routine went on into my seventh mo. The following month the Dr. said I don't know what the problem is, so continue on with your normal activities. We went to the Christmas parade and home I went into labor and called the Dr. He said I must be having a miscarriage, he sent John to the pharmacy to get medicine to help me along. Meanwhile Fred, Johns' brother and his girlfriend came to tell us they were on the way to Las Vegas to get married. John had them stay with me while he went on to get the medicine. I told Fred and Donna this is what it's like after the wedding bells stop ringing. When John got back they left and the Dr. kept helping John by phone, telling him to wrap the tissue and bring it to the office the next morning along with me as he must check me to see if I had expelled it all or if I would need a DNC. He then asked me if I wanted to know the sex and I said no, knowing that if it was a girl, I would never get over it. After I healed I had the very strong desire to have my second baby. If I had one child I might as well have the rest of my family. I thought that I was just as tied down with one so I might as well have them all. Anyway I would be a young woman when they grew up. We got pregnant the third time and gave birth to a bouncing boy. Untimely we named him Jake William. Jake was a difficult child, first I went into labor early and the Dr. gave me shots to stop the birth. I spent a day in the hospital under the watchful eyes of the nurses for any possible trouble. Then I went way over the 9 mo. pregnancy, the Dr. had to give me shots to get the birth to commence forward. I wish I knew that this was the typical way of life for us in the future. As time went on we decided that we didn't want more children so John decided to have a vasectomy, he went to the Dr. and the Dr. said no you only have two children, what if something happens to one of them? We knew the one we lost could never be replaced by another baby so we took the advice of the Dr. and gave birth to our last child another son, David Wayne Slikker. John then went on and had his vasectomy and we felt that a weight had been lifted, no more worries about pregnancy.

There was a time when Jake was about 6 mo. old that we were planning a trip to the beach. I was changing Jake and John said, where is Jon only three at the time, I said he's' outside playing and being quiet for a change. Keep in mind there is a reservoir in front of our house full of water, John said I want a snack, I heard him getting one in the kitchen. He went out the back door and I saw him in the front yard. I left Jake and followed John to the reservoir we saw nothing I started to panic and screaming Jon, Jon. John said be quiet, he listened again ran over to the metal ice chest and raised the lid, the steam and heat was almost unbearable. Out jumped the cat and John grabbed Jon and ran to the house, I called the Dr. He came to the house and checked Jon, telling us that Jon was close to dyeing the pours of his skin had ruptured due to lax of oxygen. We took him in to the Dr. the next morning they ran test and it didn't seem to affect his brain. He was going to be alright. It took this happening to make my husband admit that there was a higher power than our own that made him get up and look for his son. John said that Jon told him I called you daddy but you didn't come. He says today that is too much for him to bear knowing that was the last thought on his young son's brain. YOU WOULD'T COME

As time went on John settled into the routine of family and work. His father was an Elk and had been for many years. When we were dating we attended dances held at the Elks for the teenagers. This was an invitation to John from his father to let him sponsor John in the Elks. How could he say no? Every Tues. was Dinner for men only at the Elks and one day of the month the Women were honored with dinner. They had dances all the time and we never missed. I loved dancing so John took lessons with me and we learned to dance together from then on we never missed a dance. It was a fun time making a lot of new friends. You know making friends together, not his or not mine, our friends. Johns' friend, Ronald Kundert, Janet his wife became my best friend. Our kids were about the same age. They played together all the time, farm kids can find more things to get into. We lived five miles apart so we had to make time for them to get together. John's dad wanted John to join the bowling team for the elks. This meant that he was gone Tuesday night, and Thursday night and once a month Girl's night. Throwing in a few dance nights, when I wanted to join the Junior Women's Club and do a few of these things too, the answer was wait until the kids are older, tying the knot a little tighter around my neck.

Getting back to Jake, you know the trying one, he used to not talk I mean close to the age of 3 and 4 years. He would just grunt and point. I kept trying to get him to talk, took him to the doctor and had him checked to see if anything was wrong, no he was healthy. The Dr. suggested tranquilizers and clipping his Tongue he said he could be Tongue tied. We had that done and nothing seemed to help finally I was at my wits end and started telling him shut up Jake, I want to hear nothing from you until you say something I can understand. One day at the table he says pass the sugar and looked me right in the eye saying see there I can to talk. At the age of 16 when the school teacher asked each student what they wanted to be when they went out into the world. Jake stands and says do you want one of my business cards? He had started his own hay hauling business using the slogan he made up for himself and had it painted on his bale wagon "YOU CALL WE HAUL." This was a kid that was in a hurry to face adulthood and life at its best.

Being a farmer's wife you had to be available all the time. John was what I call a (dirt) farmer he grew crops, never had livestock of any type. John would often come into the house and ask me for help doing some chore on the ranch. Quite often he would ask me to guide the tractor thru the field while they put pipe in the field. He said it would be just a couple of rows, which always meant a half a day or so.

He would ask for help chopping weeds in the cotton, places the plane couldn't get into. I felt after all you are used to doing this you only have done it most of your life. I felt a lot of resentment as he knew how much I hated farm work. Well I loved going to the horse races, one day he requested my help chopping weeds in the cotton, telling me if I would help him with this 60 acre block he would take me to the races. One of the farm salesman happened by and he stopped, getting out of his car, he came over to me and said "Mrs. Slikker what are you doing out here in the fields" I quickly explained to him that John said after I weeded all sixty acres he would take me to the races, I never got there. Of course I had to be very dramatic and turning in a complete circle pointing at the fields as I was telling my story of "woe is me". John's father always irrigated the fields using the ditch and iron pipe. My father always used siphon pipe. John and his father decided that they would give this a try, I had to show them the correct way to get them running. It made me feel very superior.

When our oldest son was about nine years old, I wanted to do more with my life than just being a wife and mother. I had a deep need to be somebody. Lately everything I wanted to do John would say wait until the kids are older. That worked for awhile, I wanted to become friends with Betty Thome she and her husband Eddie lived with their two boys in the farm house that we lived in before we had the new house built. John said no, as her husband worked for his father, I had to keep ignoring her for quite some time, our kids went to school together. Since her husband was an employee, John felt we should not become close to the help. At this point he seemed to forget how I was raised that we were all the same my family had always been on the labor side of the ditch. One day here she came carrying two sweet potato pies. She said lets' have a snack and get acquainted, the kids had so much fun together, at least we always knew where they were, her house or mine. From that day on we never went to town alone, Betty and I with five little boys in tow. We took them out for dinner and taught them the manners for being in a restaurant. Other days we were off to the movies, we would tell the kids to be quite and make no noise. We took our own refreshments and when the kids finished their cokes you could hear the cans rolling down the aisle or stairs. So much for being quiet, you are not supposed to bring snacks into the theater. Jon and Mike were the same age and grew close as they enjoyed the same things. John and I started the 4H in our area because the kids that were old enough for High School had no way or anyone to help them raise a steer for the fair and be able to take on the responsibility for purchasing the animal and feeding it, training it and grooming it for the fair. The hard part was selling the animal and learning to let it go. These kids always fell in love with their animals and they knew that it would be slaughtered for someone's table. John had won numerous awards for Grand Champion Steer at the Kern Co. Fair and also had shown at the State Fair in Sacramento.

Ronnie was the oldest one and finished high school. He earned a scholarship for a trade school in Electronics in Las Vegas he has made his living in radios. Mike went on to Texas and into the field of refrigeration; this is what he has done all these years.

After about nine years of marriage I wanted to do more with my life than being a farmer's wife and the mother of three boys. It was such a traumatic thing that it caused the biggest fight we ever had. Since we lived on the farm John just had to walk out the door and he was at work. As our fight escalated he shouted I have to go to work. I'm saying if you go through that door I'll not be here when you come home. He yelled if you are not here when I come home you are not coming back. I'm yelling I have no intention of coming back I'm going out as I came in, a free agent and further more you are keeping the kids. This stopped him in his tracks. Apparently this was a horse of another color. He didn't go to work we have laughed about this for fifty years. Yes he did let me look for work.

Now tell me what I was going to do for a job, I had never done anything except work in the fields for my dad, part time worker at a drive-in hamburger joint and a part time secretary at the college. Not much on my résumé. John and I had these friends Ray and Sue Goodman. Sues' mom Betty had a dress shop so I decided to start there after all I grew up behind a sewing machine and I knew the basics of clothing and mending. I bet you are wondering what I did about the boys at home, Jon was nine, Jake 6 years and David was only 4. Well their father stepped up to the plate and took care of Jon and Jake keeping them with him in the field, and David I put in Nursery School. It all seemed to be well taken care of the kids all had us to themselves, no baby sitters. Betty gave me a job she took me on shopping trips to buy clothing for the store. She did all of her shopping at the discount stores where they sold overcuts and slow moving styles. Remember I knew nothing about this business, as I was learning Betty kept talking like she needed a partner as she was not able to really finance a good business. I'm all ears and more than ready to jump at the chance of being a partner in the dress business. For $1,500.00 I could own half of the business. We agreed that we would take no salaries until we were up and making a good profit. In a few short months Betty said she needed to take money as they couldn't make it on her husband's salary. I relented and Betty is now drawing a salary and my money is going back into the business. A few months later again she needed a raise, in my mind this was not going to work out. I told Betty since I put up the $1,500 and she put up nothing I thought she should call it a sale to me. Ultimately she agreed. Eventually I became friends with other dress shop owners and found a rewarding way of doing business in this field.

I learned that to make this work you had to offer the customer something that she couldn't get at any other shop. Free alterations with your purchase, personal fitting by an expert seamstress, ME!! When I went to market I would buy things especially for special customers, they could come up with a one of a kind at Slikkers. I also gave personal time for the business women in Bakersfield, some would call the shop early and ask is the coffee pot on? Yes is the answer, good I'll come by before work have coffee and check your stock and come back after work and try it on and get it fitted, if I did this today can I have it by the weekend? Yes was the answer again. This meant I put in long hours I met a lot of professional women this way and started doing fashion shows for the different organizations in town. I used to be the standby show for the Ann Guther Show, when her show got snowed in and couldn't get over the mountain she would call and ask could I do a show for her on the air. Yes I would answer and would call all of my shop models and have them meet me at the TV station, I knew their sizes and what would look good on each of them, I pulled the show and commentated it for her, it saved her hour and earned me lots of points. Another example of personal service is I had a customer and I didn't carry her size, her son was graduating from Medical School in Hawaii. She wanted new clothes and would be gone for a week. This lady did not know how to coordinate a travel wardrobe, I went shopping at different stores around town and put together a workable wardrobe, called her she loved it all I did the alterations needed and made a list of what she should wear each day and how to interchange it so that she had a different look each day. She paid for the clothes, the only money I made was what I charged for the alterations but I made a customer for the rest of her life. One time I had one of my biggest shows of my career it was at night time and involved different stores. I closed and rushed home to get dinner for the family I was in the middle of it when the phone rang and the nursery school principle asked wasn't anyone going to pick up David? Oh my gosh I had forgotten David, I rushed back to town and picked him up and then back to town for the show, we only lived about 12 miles away. What a day that was and David is now 50 years old and still today remembers mama left me at school.

My business grew so that I was doing four fashion shows a month (1 a week) ultimately this grew into having my own show on fashion for two seasons in daytime TV. I did trunk showings this is previewing the coming fashions for the next season. These shows were taped in my living room by the white rock fire place. For one of my Christmas shows the Santa did not show up, who has a Christmas show with no Santa, I went out into the field and made John come in to be our Santa. Of course he has no work to do in the fields. I got him all dressed and the show started, it was being taped, The models would show the clothes and I commentated, John patted his knee and had each model sitting on his lap. After all he should have a good time too. As I did different types of shows John modeled for me quite often, I did a wedding show for a Bridal Shop and John played the groom. Another event that I furnished a show was for Buck Owens Cancer Golf Tournament. They wanted

Bess Myerson to commentate my show and I refused to have her do it. I could see the models getting mixed up and with her reading the show talking about all the wrong fashions. I knew my fashions and if there was a mix-up I could fix it on the spot. Hosting this show meant that I had to host the celebrities at a dinner the night before. Well Charlie Pride was to be there, I saw this fellow and went up to him saying hello Charlie oh my god it was not him to my dismay it was John Amos. Comes dinner time and I have to find my place at the table oh I have found it who am I to host? It's John Amos, he was not happy about it either, when I saw him I said hello Charlie trying to make a joke out of it, he was quiet all evening. Close to the end of the evening Charlie Pride came in, John jumped up and said Charlie I want to see you on the stage. It seems that the town of Bakersfield thinks we all look alike you have hair, I don't all the while staring at me, you sing and I act. Complete embarrassment face turning red as a beet.

During this time a friend of mine knew about this venture that for $5,000.00 we could join this sub-chapter S and be partners in purchasing this property on Mt. Vernon for building a shopping center. That was cheap enough so I talked John into doing this. As months went by I heard nothing and later found out that all of the other investors never came up with their share of money. I would have to either lose my money or take over the project. Lose $5,000 I will not so instead I went 150,000.00 in debt. This is how I met George and Gwen Moss, they owned the property. Gwen became a customer a customer of mine. I had the vision of making a shopping center for the female to spend the day and entertain her friends. A restaurant with gourmet food, shoe store, leather and jewelry store and a patio where a fashion show could go on while they dined was all in my vision. Later after selling the shop Gwen gave me a job working for her and George. They taught me how to do their books and track their inventory. At this time they were in the business of building surveillance equipment for stores and police departments. George taught me to Sauder mother boards. They also allowed me to make payments on the property. I rented it out at $2,500 a month and eventually sold some of it off to pay off the Mosses. Using the rent money I bought property in Cayucos, CA. When that was paid off we borrowed enough money to build a tri-plex. We had a management co handle the rent for the vacation renters. We more or less kept one for our own use. One time they rented the whole place to some college students for their spring break, they had a word of mouth party and my neighbors called me and told me that I should be there as quick as I could make it. They had the furniture out of the apartments into the parking lot just having a great time. Another time they rented the whole place to a raga band, after that I couldn't stand to stay there anymore and we sold the place and purchased another ranch in Arvin, Ca. Now I was without a beach house and I felt lost as this was one of the places in this world that I felt whole and complete, especially since I had joined the Cayucos Art Association. At the time I didn't know it was not going to take me anywhere.

After I sold the shop I tried to retire and be with John and the kids, it was hard to get work out of my system so I took a job as a buyer for another shop. This also led me into doing all of the alterations for this store, I was getting tired.

John Brock owner of Brocks Department Store called me one day and asked if I would take a seat on the Bakersfield College Board, they were thinking of opening a department for Fashion Merchandizing. Would I help them put this together? I agreed to do this; I got to work with some of the same teachers that I had when I went to school there. We introduced buying for a store, marketing the product, how to pick your clientele, the things to watch for from potential shop lifters, handling money. Banking and making payroll. Doing the books to track inventory and sales, cash and charge sales, how to check for counterfeit bills and stolen checks. The most important is startup capital. This should cover rent, payroll, fixtures, inventory, insurance and cash to cover at least at best six months worth. All the while you are hoping to not have to touch the value of the last three month's worth of cash. My advice to all young business people is do not buy another persons' business start your own, you have no guarantee the business part of the deal will stay with you. When they charge for the business, it doesn't mean that their customers will stay with you and they always want to overcharge for this part of the sale. Do your own research. Remember my grandmothers' saying Nothing Ventured, Nothing Gained. You will always wonder what you could have done on your own.

One of the most fun periods of our life together was when I purchased a 57 Chevy Bel-Air for John for Christmas. We had been told about this car in Arvin, John had over the years cried the boo hoos over selling his original and had always wanted to get the original one back, but that was not going to happen. One day I decided to look at the car in Arvin, it was in good shape, but it would not be the way he wanted it to be, it had been made into a Hot Rod, bucket seats and all. I knew it would all have to be changed. This would add more expense to the project. I decided to buy it and I had the owner agree to deliver it Christmas morning with a big bow on top. The same afternoon John came home for lunch and said I have a free afternoon, I think I'll drive to Arvin and take a look at that Chevy Jake keeps talking about. If it's in good condition I think I'll buy it and fix it up, Jake says it has some issues. I told him no you cannot buy that car, I put my foot down hard on solid ground and thought I could con him out of the car instead he turned to me and said who do you think you are telling me what I can and cannot do? I shouted because I bought it this morning thanks so much for that Christmas surprise. They are delivering it Christmas morning. He replied can we go get it now? Sure and at this point I needed another plan for his Christmas. We seem to think of things at the same time, he said at that moment so for my Christmas we can have it restored. OK

Now he had read in the paper about the 55 56 57 Chevy club. We called and went to a meeting, there we met good friends, people from all walks of life but they all loved their Chevy's. This group took rides and had picnics. Once a year they held a Car Show donating proceeds for different charities, since our club president was Joe Boren, who was a captain in the Fire Dept. The club voted to donate each year to the camp for burn victims, children who were severally burned and would have a hard time in life. At this same time I got my first car also, 1950 Ford Business Coup, later I added a 56 T Bird with the port holes. I had a lot of fun with these people. I could get John to take me into some of the show rooms, Oh my God there was this beautiful Model A Ford. A 1939, black and green complete with the rumble seat. Oh John can we get it no he says you already have two cars, I got in it and started it and it was so smooth for an old car. I said I'll take it, the sales man asked what name should he make the title out to me I said, while I was walking around the car I noticed it had two tail pipes, I asked why two? He told John he wondered how long it would take me to notice that I was about to buy a Hot Rod capable of going from a stop to 60miles an hour in 60 seconds. This made my blood flow a little harder. I told him to put it in my name since John said no I couldn't have it the salesman looked at John then I said oh put his name on it to as he is the one paying for it. Our group was planning a get together at shopping center parking lot to plan an outing to the lake near the coast. We asked can Dorothy join us with her new 1939 Model A. only if she can keep up with us. Ok, that night when I was coming into the lot they all said ok she's in. The Chevy's and one Ford had a very nice outing.

Oh listen to me carry on as if I was the wisest person around. I am still trying to retire I get a call from one of my dress shop owner friends asking me to work for her. I said I'm trying to be around when John has time to go to our house at the lake. So I could help you out once in awhile, but not on a regular basis and I would have to work for clothes. She says no I need to pay you, finally I agreed to help her get caught up. Her daughter Lois worked there she was an artist ah ha here comes my art back into my world. Lois proceeded to tell me she taught art at the Mize Art Gallery in East Bakersfield would I like to take a class from her? I said no as I had lost all of my confidence many years ago. I have had no contact with art in any form for at least 15years. Lois kept after me for quite some time I kept talking about it to John and procrastinating about building up enough courage to plunge into it. I knew if I wanted to be good at it I would have to stick to it long enough to see if I still liked it. Lois promised to start me out with something simple. OK I give in teach me how to paint. I didn't know one medium from another, she said don't worry about supplies I will have everything you need there.

John said take those classes you keep talking about. I told Lois ok lets' teach me what I need to know all the while thinking I can't do this. I was already taking cake decorating classes and doing pretty good. This means that I can take direction and learn something about my unknown talents. It took quite some soul searching for me to give myself permission to try again after so long. Between cake decorating, candy making and art I now had a full schedule. Also I was available when John and the boys needed me.

Ok my first class, what will be my project? A tree with a fence stream and land this shouldn't be too difficult for a beginner. We painted the sky and then a dark brown tree we then used a process called a wipe out using turpentine to remove some of the dark brown forming knot holes and texture to the tree. Next came the land which we did in green and learned how to make grass next came the stream separating them we put in a fence, I must say my wire was quite thick, but it was my first master piece. Next came my painting of a road coming over a hill with weeds in the middle allowing me to make ruts in the road, a clump of trees on each side with birds in the sky. My worst piece was the pier in the fog. My kids always say do you still have that god awful painting of the boat in the fog? Answer is yes. I never knew if I was learning anything or not, the paints were always mixed for the painting, we did and used what we were told to do. I call this monkey see monkey do. I had at least eight classes before Lois had us do a black and white. This is what I should have been shown in the first class, maybe then I would have realized what it was all about. The dept or perception in the painting, what to do to make these things happen. Lights and darks tell you everything, how to place shadows, they tell you where the light is coming from, colors that make a painting cool or hot. So much to learn, every once in awhile a traveling artist would come to the gallery and give a weekend class. You could do such a good painting when you study under different teachers. My first one under the traveling artist situation was a light house, cliff and trees. It was set in a sunset that was quite dark.

My life continued on as it always had just as if it was written somewhere. Taking classes decorating cakes and painting my master pieces. It was known that I was a good seamstress and I was soon asked to be a judge for the sewing at the Kern Co. Fair, I was quite honored to do this. Also the same year Lois talked me into entering some of my paintings in the fair. To my surprise I took second place in the armature class, the following year I took Honorable Mention, I was then taunted that I couldn't even place in the local fair. This almost made me want to quit painting, but I hung in there. Getting back to being a judge in the sewing category of the fair, it soon got around that I knew what I was talking about and was soon asked to Judge the State Make it With Wool Contest. Now this was really an honor that was bestowed on me. A state wide sewing Judge, granny would be proud of me now. Granny was the one who taught me to sit behind a sewing machine and make some of my own clothes, I left grannies house at the age of eight. As I have said before I made almost all of my clothes. After I had been married for a few years I had purchased my first dress from a store, it was pink checkered spaghetti strap dress, I was standing at the green stamp line in the store to redeem my stamps holding Jon I felt my dress just spread apart. I was so humiliated rushing from the store to home, needless to say I never purchased another dress for a long time years in fact.

It seemed like all John did was work, we never got to leave the ranch for anything anyway that is how I felt. John and I decided that we would buy a lot at the lake and put a mobile home on it just to be able to be away but close enough if he needed to get back home. We purchased a lot in Bodfish in the Lake Isabella area. Later we went to the bank and financed a mobile home and it was already to go. I met John at the mobile home lot and he was sitting on the step of the one we had picked out, he said to me should we do this? I got so mad and said hell no that's why we got the loan to put nothing on the lot. He could tell this was not going to work this time I was now asserting my will over his, he could tell I was becoming my own person. The first year we were able to use it 76 days, a far cry from never getting away from the farm. It was close enough that I could go up with the children and some of their friends and spend time at the park and river in Kernville. Life was good. John made friends with the neighbor Sonny and they went fishing a lot together. On one of these fishing trips they were surprised by a rattle snake, John said it was about even with their heads, Sonny jumped into action and beat the snake until it was dead, John was sure wary of it as it was riding in the back of the pickup. The story they had to tell was a mighty big tale, but they had the proof to show us. His wife Lucille and I got acquainted and talked a lot about crafts and such. During the second year we had this horrible wind and dust storm, we lost our power and had no water, some people smothered to death in the storm, ones that were caught in their cars. It filled the canals with dirt it brought the stories of the dust bowl back to life in my memories. I took the children and we lived at the mobile home in Bodfish until things turned back to normal. After another year John said let's build on the mountain. I want to experience the changing of the seasons. We could sell the mobile and build a house. I answered we don't sell the mobile until we have a lot on the mountain. I knew if we did it his way there would be no other home built. We browed money from his Uncle Kampe and purchased a lot. We then sold the mobile home paying his Uncle back and enough to build an A frame cabin. It had all the things I would want in a home for retirement. We even bought a two person hot tub. I loved it and so did John. He could drive down the mountain and fish in the Kern River, in the winter we learned to snow ski. I was learning to ski at the age of 42, I was so stupid. It finally lost its luster when the kids came up and I wound up staying at the cabin babysitting all the time. They were all enjoying my paradise. We now had a place in each of the places that I ever vacationed at as a child. It's funny how things turn out. All the while I kept painting and taking classes, I felt my work was getting better as I kept at my craft, anyway I felt it was good enough to give a piece of my work for a prize at the party in the Lodge. On weekends Jake usually had a group playing for the weekend crowd. Being mom I was quite pleased with him, he even trained his dog to be on stage with him and sing when he started playing.

One day our house got broken into and the only things stolen were my skis. Thank god the insurance paid for them and I never had to ski again. We learned on the road in front of our house. The next morning we got up early and headed up the hill, John wanted to beat the crowd and be on the slope alone. He finally got his skis on and headed for the hill started down the hill gaining speed he thought that he had better use the snow plow technique that he had been taught for slowing down or coming to a stop WHAT NOT SLOWING DOWN, NOT STOPPING! He finally got down and came walking back up I asked how it was, he replied F…THIS SHIT this is not for me. He didn't realize the snow was frozen until the sun came up. I never got good enough to leave the Bunny hill, but John did. So when my skis were stolen I was a happy camper I was perfectly good with the warming hut and hot chocolate.

Let me tell you about each one of my sons, Jon, is the oldest and a model child, always doing the things that he was told to do. I must have made him his brothers' keeper as even today he looks after them. When Jon was about 9 yrs old we took the kids on a trip, it was one of our first road trips and I think the last, we went up to Canada, along the way the Worlds' Fair was in full swing. John took us all on a helicopter ride and Jon fell in love with flying at that very moment and it's all I heard about for years. John took care of the kids while I worked so they learned how to drive and operate the equipment pulling the disk and landplane around the field, leaving their dad free to do other chores. Jon was the first one performing these tasks and Jake would not be left behind. He spent hours riding with his brother. It wasn't long before Jake was at the controls himself. They would harvest the Milo and run the cultivator through the cotton. Jon's love of flying was by now driving me crazy, it was always let me take lessons. I would answer I didn't raise you just to have you kill yourself in a plane. After Jon graduated from high school I told him ok if you really want to fly now you can. That day he soloed, Jon had been taking lessons behind my back. His real love was Helicopters he bought his first flying machine a gyrocopter. It took about a mile of running down the road before it would lift off. Next he purchased a helicopter and one of the crop dusters taught him the mechanics of flying it. One day while we were gone Jon was working on the helicopter and got his finger in the blade someway and almost ripped it from his hand. After it healed he could never straighten it again. He kept the first helicopter for quite a while then sold it and purchased a Hiller Helicopter in this one he learned to crop dust with it. To be able to get the time and get a job flying, he had to go to Mississippi to get in the hours. When he came back he got hired by this co to fly for them. Today Jon and his wife Monica own the co. that gave him his first chance at flying for a living the biggest crop dusting co in California. You never know what it is that your kids will get themselves into. Jon and Monica have three sons also. Jon Edwin Jr., Dustin Ryan, Benn Slikker. Jon is working with his mom and dad in the flying business, Dustin is a paramedic for the city of San Diego, CA and Benn is a Captain in the Air Force he teaches student pilots to fly the C130's the cargo plane a big Multi Engine plane.

Now it's Jake's turn to make his mark on life, as I said before even as a small child he gave us so many problems. When you went to punish Jake he would only stare you down and would never cry. Not until you made him go to his room would he shed a tear, he had to be alone. This behavior drove his dad to the breaking point, he would say this kid hates me, if a kid would kill his parents this is the one that would do it. Little did his dad know Jake, he was the most sensitive child we had. When Jake started dating almost every girl he dated he thought he was in love with. Thus he married three times. He was musical, playing the sax in band in high school, and later the drums, organ and guitar. He always had a band and they played Country Western Music. He would get jobs in different bars, when he turned 21 we went to the bar where he was playing, they asked for our drink order and turned to Jake and said the same as usual Jake, he answered yes. All the time he was employed there they thought he was old enough to be there. Not until that night. Jakes third wife was a groupie, when she met Jake she knew he was in music. He had an offer to travel to Europe for touring and she had a fit, later they went to Vegas with her father and he and his girlfriend got married, she and Jake thought this was a great idea and did the same. Later on after a year or so she made him give up his music. Jake had been driving truck and his boss got him hooked on drugs to keep him on the road and work long hours, Denise, Jake's wife was also on drugs getting started on them by her father and cousins. To make the long story short they had a child, naming him Jake Jr. He had been born with so many problems his bladder was out of his body. It required extensive surgery, all the way to the Children's Hospital Jake saying and crying why, does it always happen to me? I told him that it didn't happen to him it happened to Jake Jr. It was a very trying time all the while I stayed with them in the hospital. Later when they could take him home Jake wanted to be the one to take care of him, I had a hard time getting him to go to work. It seemed like the baby was a good baby never crying or fussing. After awhile when he was sleeping Jake thought he was too quiet and checked on him, he had died. At this point I too felt that life was dealing Jake a hard hand. The helicopter ambulance came and took little Jake to the hospital. Jake called us and we met him at the hospital. The cops were drilling him as though he was a criminal. After a while Jake and Denise had two more boys, Tyler and William Slikker

Jake and Denise stayed married and got heaver into the drug scene. This finally broke up their marriage. Jake didn't show up for court and Denise got everything almost even the kitchen sink. Jake was ordered to pay child support and Denise went on welfare.

Eventually all of this life style put Jake in jail for drugs. He got a year and later was sent to the labor farm on Lerdo Hwy. He served six months and was sent to a half way house for another six months. After the half way house he was on probation, they took away his driver's license and he couldn't work as he was a truck driver. How was he going to make a living legally? With no way to support himself, he came to us in Pahrump, NV. The probation officer o.k.'s this move and we paid the fine of $2,400.00 he later puts a bench warrant out on Jake for his arrest for breaking parole one week early about leaving Kern Co. and living with us. While he was in Nevada they did not enforce the warrant and when he went back to Bakersfield, they picked him up and he had to serve another six months. The system seems to enjoy making the life of a troubled man all the more difficult. While our own American citizen is down they take away all of his rights and driving license. At the same time they are willing to give illegal's all of the rights that belong to our citizens. With no license how was he supposed to work, he is a truck driver for god's sake during all this time Jake had Tyler and William with him almost half of the time. As of today Jake is working the best that he can and living in a fifth wheel, with his cats. Tyler is now applying for the Police Academy and he has finished the schooling for the police with flying colors. William is at this time the lead guitarist for the band The Aviators. I am proud of them both as they seem to be making a good life for themselves in a drug free environment. Needless to say Jake told Tyler he could practice his police holds on his dad. One day when I went to visit him at Lerdo, I told him that the name of a Physiatrist had been given to me so that when he got out we could all see him and maybe figure out what was going so wrong in his life. He said mom why do you need a physiatrist it is me that has screwed up my life. I asked Jake do you think this was my plan for your life as I carried you for nine months, being a druggie and in Jail. I could see for the first time the look that came over his eyes that this made a lot of sense to him, he has been straight every since. We love this boy and I don't think he ever thought so.

David Wayne was our third son and was the baby of the family. When David was about two years old he always insisted on wearing a hat. When one was not always available he substituted a Tupperware bowl for outdoor play. The slikker boys always played outside on the farm. Each of them doing their own things and setting their paths for the future. One day I went outside to check on them and found them under the tree in the sand box playing with their farm tools, I guess their clothes caused too much constriction as they were all three playing in the nude pushing and making the sounds of plowing and pulling rows for their farm on the sand. Butts in the air showing the world what they were all made from. Jake was the one that couldn't stay in his clothes. When we went to the beach he always took off his training pants before hitting the water. What will I ever do with this one! John had a unique way to water our lawn. He hooked the pipe to an outlet on the main line turned the water on to the yard. This made the house an island in the center of the place, you could look out and see all the boys running and playing and having the greatest time, what a cool way for our hot summer days. It was the day and age that the slip and slide was being used another way to cool off. Let's not forget the hula hoop, we all got pretty good at this one that is except for dad.

David was a speed demon and became one of the best go cart racers around. One of his friends Mark Reed became a race driver. While David was in High School he built his own race car, while I was in Europe my mom whom was supposed to be taking care of the kids, let him race his car at Mesa Marine. Mom what were you thinking? David was not supposed to finish his race car let alone drive it in the adult races. Don't worry Dorothy he blew the engine in the first round, now all you have to do is go and sign the papers. OK. The next thing I knew here comes Jake flying an ultra light alone over head, yelling hi mom. My God what's next? This is the time that Jon had gotten his Gyrocopter. As David got older he worked as a pit crew member on a racers car. Our neighbor in the mountains was Rick Mears and our boys got a kick out of having to pull his car out of a snow drift. I mentioned that his good friend at the time was Mark Reed, well to tell the story on them they were out one night with my pickup and had an accident, Mark's father brought David home trying to explain that they had rolled my pickup, but it was not their fault, they weren't going that fast and lost control of the pickup. The next morning John made David show him the spot where this all took place, there were at least 85feet of skid marks before they hit the embankment and lost control and rolled the truck. John said they had to be going faster than fast to accomplish this feat. John lost respect for Jim for lying to him about the accident just to make things go easier for David with his dad. We were really just grateful that he was alright. David loved farming as much as his dad did. David is the one still active in farming for a big co. Hirschman Enterprises, he controls the planting, growing and harvesting of all the row crops for the co.

There was a time before David had his driver's license that he and Jake were out playing with the cars, Jake had his car and David my truck, they were on the freeway and decided to follow a little old woman that was alone tailgating her all the way home. They would then find another one, as they were doing this there was a drug deal going down and the truck involved was just like mine. When Jake caught up with David he saw that the cops had his brother spread eagled on the ground searching him. Jake stopped to see what was going on, the cops asked do you know this guy, Jake said yes he's my brother. The cops let David up and then told them what was happening, they told David to leave the pickup where it was as David was driving without a license, he only had a learners permit to drive with a licensed driver. Jake and David left and after the police were gone they went back and got the truck. I found out about this when one of Jakes friends asks me while I was in the grocery store, what I did to Jake. I ask about what, at this point I made him tell me.

Finally they were all out of high school and still at home, working on the farm and running around with girls and feeling their oats. One day as I was doing the family laundry I found a rubber in the dryer. I took it out and asked the ultimate question, whom does this belong? John my husband yells not mine, and one by one each says it's not mine either ok I guess it's' mine. After spending the weekend at the house in the mountains, we walked into the house to find everything a mess, David had given a party that invitation got passed by word of mouth, it was so loud, even for the farm, the neighbor called the police and they stopped the party. As I went through the house and found a pair of panties in my bed armed with that knowledge I told John we don't have any babies anymore not a nary one.

Although John and I were both working we made sure to have plenty of time to do things with the boys. John had a boat that was in his family, we took it out often and John taught all of the boys to water-ski. There were many trips to Lake Ming for boating and a picnic. My sons all married in their 20's. We saw nothing wrong with this as we were also young when we married. Jon married Monica Adel Beacherer, in time they had the three boys, Jake had married three times and had his two boys and David married Lori Elkins, and had his two daughters, later he married Heidi and they had his son Brock David, Heidi died when Brock was around four years old, today Brock is a Freshman in High School and is very active in sports. David is very happy with his life and new love Carla.

RETIREMENT AND ART

I CONTINUED TO HELP John on the farm doing the farm books and helping to attain the financing for the ranch. It just seemed like the bull was going to continue messing with our future. One day John came in and asked me to go to the Hay Growers Co. and see about selling the hay we had on the yard. There were three large stacks and it was first cutting. We were trying to make hay for horses and that type of hay had to reach 15-17% moisture and be free of weeds this was considered dry not good for dairy feed. The horses could not eat moist alfalfa it would give them gas. That morning I went to the Hay Growers and asked to speak with the buyers. A fellow came out to talk to me about my product and asked me what I had to sell. Very fine stem alfalfa hay and at 15-17%moisture for horses. Its' first cutting and not weedy. He asks "what do you want for it"? $115.00 per ton, no he says its first cutting and it is always weedy, besides we will have to take a 3% non refundable fee for the revolving fund and also a commission. This will leave you with around $99.00 per ton, this would only be the offer since we have to come and check it. I answered that I would have to talk it over with John and his dad. This is the typical way a farmer has always sold their commodities; my way was going to be new for them. John came in at noon for lunch and says did you go to the Hay Growers this morning? Yes was the reply, but you are not going to sell the hay to them. What the hell do you mean, how will we move that much hay ourselves? I will sell it some way but we are through taking what someone wants to give to get the best deal for themselves.

During the course of the day a man came to the house and asked if the hay was for sale. I told him yes and he wanted to know how much it was, I said $130.00 a ton since it had the moisture content of 17% and was fine stemmed and baled for horses. He said can I check the hay with my moisture probe? OK was the answer, he said yes it is fine stemmed and there are no weeds. I commented that my husband was the best farmer around the parts and he did his own work, the man answered it shows but I can't go $130.00 would you take $115.00? I answered it depends on how much you want to buy? Oh I'm taking all of it. He gave me his name and said he would come back and have a cashier's check for all three stacks. John came home later that evening after a long day in the fields saying did you sell any hay today? Yes I answered. How much one bale? No all of it, WHAT the hell did you give it away how much did you get? $115.00 per ton our asking price. When will they pick it up, tomorrow and they will have the money. Who was it? Williams Hay Co I answered. Damn. I said I told you that if I could sell a dress I could sell a bale of hay. This was the beginning of Slikker's Hay Co. We eventually sold hay to Universal Studios in Hollywood, their farm that supplied them the show animals and so many horse farms around the area. We made a reputation that this was the place to purchase your horse hay. Sometimes it got comical; they would come before breakfast in a Volks Wagon Jon would commence to tie a bale to the top of this small car. Some people went without eating themselves just to be able to feed their horses. There were many days that I never got dressed since the customers lined up and kept doing it all day. We finally had to purchase a truck to be able to offer the service of delivery.

Now at the same time we started our own Orange Packing Co. called Slikker's Farm and developed our own brand and label

Prtyslik California Oranges and started our gift packing business, we were in competition with Harry and David, and Hickory Farms sending gift packs in the mail. All and all I guess I did retire from the dress business. HA

Having started the gift packing business I felt that on the off season, instead of losing our customers, I should open a Country Farm Store in the mall. I made our labels and never sold a product that didn't say Slikker Farms. During the off season I still did the gift packs with the summer fruits and sausages cheese and jams and jellies. I could make a breakfast gift and one that would appeal to the men in your lives, "country picnic baskets with all the trimmings". Then when it was time for oranges we put together our catalog for the season. I managed to get a few large companies to do baskets for all of their employees. John the boys and myself worked our butts off during this time of year. John worked all day packing oranges commercially and then would help me finish up at night, the next morning before daylight we were at it again. The boys had to be in the fields early before the pickers arrived to make sure they were in the right spot, after they were picked they had to get them to the shed, Jake worked as our mechanic and helped to keep the equipment from breaking down. At this point there was not much time for me to do my art work, but I managed to paint one now and then.

Our main store was on the farm and I had a crew working there and a group working in the East Hills Mall and Later one in the Valley Plaza. I felt we had the area covered quite well. I had the large orders for baskets sent to the farm store and I personally made each and every one of them.

In the early 1990's we had a hard freeze across the country. It was so bad that it affected the entire country. By this time we had sold both farms to be able to stay on top of our work, both financially and management. The freeze was so bad that Al Roker interviewed a farmer from California early in the morning showing the ice icicles hanging from the oranges, the farmer interviewed was John and our son David. We managed to stay in business for another seven or eight years and we had another freeze that just about paralyzed the nation. This is the one that put us over the top and forced us to retire. Bankrupt that was the story in the cards for us. We licked our wounds and moved forward into the unknown.

We managed to save our home and I moved to Cayucos at the beach. I got a job at Sears in San Louis Obispo working in the clothing dept. John stayed behind and went to work for another packing co helping them set up their orange packing shed. I now had plenty of time for my art work. I rejoined the art association in Morro Bay and Cayucos. I found out that new comers were still not to be accepted as an equal. I was raised to think we were all alike and we all had our different talents and areas of expertise. Not in this world. I would attend the meetings and sit the galleries and pay the others for lessons. Once I even bought a piece of work from one of them. Nothing seemed to help me fit in so I resigned myself to do my work at home and paint as I saw fit. This worked out for us for a few years John commuting back and forth.

In the year of 2000 I talked John into selling the house at the beach, I wanted to sell and move to a place that was a little more affordable. He would fight me all the way, one day we decided to take a train trip to Reno, the ride was gorgeous, while we were passing through John turned to me and said ok lets sell the house and move to Nevada. We neither one had lived in another state other than California. After the return home we found a realtor to sell our house. I said I wanted $550,000 for it. John said we would never get that kind of money, I told him I wanted to sell it not give it away. We finally had a buyer, but there was about $10,000.00 of work that needed to be done first. We had all of the repairs completed and sold the house for 530,000. That amount paid off the bank and we moved to Pahrump, NV, we were able to build a beautiful home, paying cash for it and put money in the bank to start our life over.

One day we were in the flooring store, I happened to strike up a conversation about my art work. Gary the owner asked if I had a sample of some of my work. Out in the car I replied, John went to the car and brought back one of the paintings. Gary and his wife right on the spot said let's see what kind of a promotion we can put together and move carpet and art at the same time. Me like most artist wants more than an arm and a leg for our work, we have the tendency to price ourselves out of the market place. They came up with when a customer bought so much carpeting for their home they could pick a painting from a local artist. The artist in return would receive $100.00 per painting. The first month they moved ten paintings for me. That's a $1000.00 in my pocket. Not bad for an unknown. Its' great having people who think that my work is good. Later after this business closed I decided to see if another co. would be interested in the same type of program. I found one they also said this work should be hanging in the court house gallery. I asked whom it would be that I should be in contact with. After getting a number I called and a man by the name of Bernie answered and told me that that Friday bring some work to the court house and he would hang my work with the others. I couldn't ask for more, sure was different than at the coast.

Friday came and I showed up with three of my paintings. A couple of women came in and introduced themselves to me and explained what PAC was all about. I asked what I had to do to join the organization. They proceeded to ask what I wanted and what I expected from PAC, I said to be as busy as I can be and helpful as a bee. They then told me when the next meeting would be held and I should come and meet some of the other artist. I attended a meeting at the home of Loretta Lindell, it was the hospitality group. It was a good place to start. After this I showed my art in all of the shows. I later started teaching in my studio at home. I also had a part time job teaching at the Busy Bee, this was all younger students. One day this lady came into the shop to pick up her grandson, she stated to me that she would sure like to learn to paint, I said ok but you have to come to my studio. You can't learn here. Lenora Danielson started her first lesson, never having held a brush in her hand, the one thing is she never uttered the words I can't do this, it was always show me how. I have to admit that some of our first work was not very good. By the time she left my classes she had painted what I would have considered a masterpiece. Another student Donna Paulson never missed a class, Donna was already a good artist and she wanted to paint for therapy. I also had a string of young students, they too were pretty good artist. There was this one that wanted to do abstracts I never felt that I was the teacher for this method of painting. I soon found an Abstract artist that took this student for her own. The young girl seemed to flourish on her own with the guidance of her new teacher.

As I mentioned I had young students so when I decided to show her work and mine at the Art & Sol show, she sold more of her paintings than I did, but too she self-marketed herself to her parents and grandparents friends.

It was during this show I met the artist Doris Smith. She came to my booth and said that she and I would be good friends, I asked why, she answered we paint alike two peas in a pod. This was the year of 2003 and today it's 2017 it's been a good friendship.

Doris is the artist that got me into the Las Vegas Art Convention we took classes with Johnnie Lillidahl, Bill Bayer and Robert Warren. The first year I painted with Johnnie and painted the Water Maiden, then later during the convention I painted with Bill Bayer, we did a lagoon and mountain point. During our break I visited the convention floor and looked all the art booths over, coming to this booth with Robert Warren. His work took my breath away. All of a sudden I wanted to have my work look like this artists work. As I was looking over his art I saw his sign telling you that you could become certified in his method of painting. It would take three years of hard work to become certified. He gave the classes in Ohio, a long way to travel away from home. When I got home I told John all about these classes and how much I wanted to take them. He agreed to go along with the idea ok now tell him these classes are in Ohio and lasted a week at a time. Finally he agreed and off to another journey. We flew went by train and drove to the classes. This was one hell of a vacation, doing what I loved, I passed the final and became certified with Robert Warren.

I felt so smart, smug and sure of myself, I applied to be a teacher at the convention in Las Vegas. I was accepted and decided my golfer would be my first project. This was the year 2009 that all of a sudden I was having hard time breathing. John took me to the Dr. and they left me sitting out in the waiting room, the nurse for my Dr. came by and I told him I couldn't breathe, he said follow me. He took my oxygen level and said you can't breathe and proceeded to put me on oxygen while I waited for the Dr. to check me out. The next week we went to California to a wedding I kept telling John what awful tasting food they were serving. A little later I asked John to leave and the next morning we left for Nevada. As we were coming into Pahrump I said let's stop and eat as I don't feel like cooking. We stopped and as we were leaving the restaurant I starting feeling sick.

By the time we got home I was sick to my stomach. I couldn't stop throwing up and John took me in to Las Vegas to the Emergency Room. Dr. Lazani was on call and he happened to be the type of Dr. for the kidneys. He thought I had gallstones and proceeded to try to make me pass them. No gallstones so he inserted a stint to the bladder, this did not help either, after doing this procedure a couple more times he decided that he would use the water method of bursting the stones. Didn't work, next he did a procedure to remove the urine that had thickened to a paste. This kept me in the hospital because at one point I went out on them, when I came to the Dr. was hitting me in the face I said that hurts. They put me in ICU for twelve days with an infectious disease Dr. I had become so infected that I was going septic. John notified Doris and she being the type of person she was did my class for me at the convention. After the year the Dr. told us that it would be better for me to let him fix my deformed kidney (this was the final diagnosis)this was not letting the kidney completely clean itself and get rid of all the urine. I consented and today I thank Dr. Lazine for saving my life.

After getting better I gave a class at the convention painting my wolf. It was so popular and was one I painted at the kitchen table on my own in Cayucos. I had a sell-out of seats for the class a whopping 37 students. I was in my glory John helped he collected the money and sold brushes for me. From that class I had a student that wanted me to stay in her vacation condo and give her lessons for a week. It was wonderful. I encouraged her to follow Robert to his different locations and she could paint with the master herself. Another one of my projects was the horse Roper on The Beach I gave a private class at the clubhouse here in my community, about fifteen came and it was also a good class. Later I applied for more classes, when I turned in my photo's they said I had them on my website so therefore could not teach a painting that has been published, having them on my website was considered published. Shortly after that I got sicker and sicker. I have now given up the Las Vegas Convention.

When Doris wanted to go and paint with Gary Jenkins in their home in Carson City Nevada I jumped at the chance to join her. Gary is the master of floral. We painted for a week with Gary and his wife Kathryn helping us in the background. It was one of the most memorable events of my life.

Later came leaving my realm of comfort, applying for representation in Galleries out of my home place. I was now using my computer for my art and having had a web site created I was starting to get some notice from different galleries about my work The Agora Gallery in NYC notified me asking if I would like to apply. I checked them out and found that they showed mainly abstract art and I didn't feel that it was the venue for me so I tabled the offer. I just continued doing what I do best painting and teaching art. After a couple of years I got the inquiry again from the Agora Gallery. This time I took the time to check them out and found that they were showing more contemporary work. With this information in hand I contacted them and checked out their site and listened to what they had to offer me in the way or representation. They said four months in the gallery my virtual wall and website with their gallery and also a presentation in their book, Art is Spectrum. They showed me when I was a featured artist with the Henderson Art Association. They featured my Golfer and wrote a blurb about me and my work. This was the first time of anything like this for me. I also wanted to be at the champagne reception. John would not go so I asked my son Jon to go with me. He called me the next day, he and Monica would both take me as my Christmas present. They got us the most beautiful room on 8th street I soon learned that it was centrally located to all of the things I wanted to see. On our first day we found all of the galleries I wanted to visit, most of all the Agora Gallery. The following day we saw the city by tour bus. The Statue of Liberty and so many more of the sites of interest that night was the reception at the gallery, we no sooner got thru the door than a couple of artist from Italy started talking to me and took me by the arm to see their work and then they would check out mine. As I was being kidnapped by these artists my son said but mom, be quiet Jon I am having a good time. I was Alice in Wonderland that night oh so magical. I loved being able to talk to a lot of people that loved art. These artist were from all around the world. They all wanted to know where I get my inspiration from, showing them the subjects of my art I proudly pointed out that my inspiration was my grandchildren. I was showing my grandson golfing in the sunset and he was also the wake boarder. One man came by and asked if I was the Artist and I answered yes, he explained that he was an art teacher at one of the High Schools there in NYC continuing on he said it's such a pleasure to see real art these days. I felt so honored. Monica's niece that lives there came with her family; they presented me with a bouquet of yellow roses, such an honor.

The next day Jon and Monica took me on the sleigh ride in the park. I had told Jon that was one of the things I wanted to do in New York. I saw the kids' ice skating on a pond, you know only the one in the movies or the books were ever shown. Times Square was a site for sore eyes. The kids skating and the tree lighted just like on TV. Now comes the time to board the plane and head back to Nevada.

Now back to reality I have submerged myself back to work in the studio. I paint at least two paintings a week if I work all the time. Most of the time I complete three a month it depends on the classes I teach. My students would being into class what they wanted to paint since I work one on one I painted the same painting explaining what brushes to use to create different things, what paints to mix to reach the value of the painting they envisioned. Before the end of the year I receive another call from NYC

I received a call from Amsterdam Whitney Gallery. Would I be interested in showing for four months with them and I would have to sign a one year contract. They were only interested in my Floral and Still Life's. The Still Life looks so much like the masters in the museums. What an honor and I agreed to the contract. I sent the paintings and they stayed for the full four months, this brought other inquiries to my site and work. It seemed that my work was much more popular on the east coast than here.

Later I started getting inquiries from different art books that have been presented by another Artist. To make their books you have to have your work judged by an art critic. If it passes you are then considered printable material. I was first approached by Art Quench Magazine. Be inspired and get art quenched is the motto of the magazine. This book was founded by Stacie Gates. Her quote is that love, hope, clarity and awareness are the key ingredients to a successful and happy journey in art.

Art Tour International, ATIM'S TOP 60 MASTERS OF CONTEMPORARY ART contacted me and asked to send work so that they could have them judged. I obliged knowing full well that I was not in the category of work yet. I sent in 4-6 photo's for the judging. The e-mails started coming telling me that I had made the Top 60 artist being considered as masters in contemporary art. Asking me to be part of the magazine and they would be contacting me to do a video of me talking about my work and why I wanted to be an artist. Only all my life… My work was presented in the 2016 and again in 2017. Curated by the internationally acclaimed art personality Viviana Puello, editor in chief of Art Tour International Magazine, the publication spotlights top talent from a broad range of artistic forms. Over the years, many internationally renowned artists have been showcased in the pages of this state-of-the-art publication. Including Fernando Botero, Lorenzo Quinn among many others. It has been a thrilling ride all of the recognition of me and my work. It was after the Art Tour Magazine articles that I began getting invitations from the European Countries. There was no way for me to travel to these places or even afford the expense of sending my work. Instead I would send photos and they would show them in their virtual galleries. They were also included in the magazines for the different shows. This was the way that my work was presented in the world galleries. The shows were in Japan, Italy, and Holland. My work is well received.

I was noticed in Berlin Germany they produced their first book in 2017. A quote from Gabriela Caranfil she is the curator of this book known as THE FIRST BERLINER ART BOOK. He who is called to make art has the supreme ability and privilege to materialize the invisible and the unknown, and to become the breath and the soul of eternal answers of the humanity. A new publication that I made it into was the CONTEMPORARY ART OF EXCELLENCE.

Top 100 Contemporary Masters, book curate by Despina Tunberg. Now I am being asked to present work to them, do I think I could pass their stiff set of rules for art. Why not give it a try, all you have to do is send in a few pictures, if they turned you down how can it hurt. Remember Granny saying nothing ventured nothing gained. Ok here goes I will cross my fingers as this is for the Top 100 artist to make the masters in contemporary art. A few weeks went by and I heard nothing from them and then I received an e-mail saying congratulations you have received representation in the top 100 contemporary masters, there are no words to describe how I felt. My feet never hit the ground for weeks. The first thing I wanted to do was call Doris but by this time I felt like I was bragging all the time, I have to stop doing it I could be hurting someone's feelings. I waited almost a year for my copy of the book to arrive. Finally it did arrive and now I had proof of my success. Later I received an invitation to show in Las Vegas at The Museum of Fine Art with the top 100 world masters of contemporary art. The show would last for four months and I could bring along two guests. John and my good friend Doris Smith would be my esteemed guest. John bought us both a corsage to wear that night. I had another guest Debbie Shultz and her husband. You see I was so excited about these honors that I had to sit right down and write a book. Debbie helped me along as she worked as my auditor. The honors bestowed upon me made me so proud that I named the book MY ART WALK TO THE CONTEMPORARY MASTERS. In this book I showed some of my early work before taking lessons from Robert Warren, during my lessons, and later on in my career. One of the hardest paintings to show was the first one painted the boat in the fog. I don't know how this book was received, but it has brought me even more recognition.

Next came an inquiry for me to enter the competition for the Inspiration INTERNATIONAL ART BOOK Contemporary Masters Collection, this was another step up in prestige, I was making a name in the Art World. This book was published in London, England. I made it for the 2016 and 2017 editions and have been invited for 2018. Every time I open these books I get the feeling of such pride. Especially when I open the book to my pages and see it says International Artist Dorothy Slikker United States of America. Such pride.

Being recognized by the TV medium came next an interview with Jim Masters and Doug Lu Ellen on CUTV news. At a later date they came to Nevada from NY to interview me on camera and show my art work and art studio. I couldn't have been more honored.

Strathmore's Who was another honor, being named as one of the top business women in the USA in the field of art. They honored me with my picture shown on the building in NYC Times Square. Also I was honored with the first page in their book for the year of 2017.

LIFE GOES ON

I MAY SOUND LIKE I think my life is over, it's only beginning as far as I can think of it. I have had a life to be proud of and I have had many experiences to think about. Especially writing this book has made me reflect on all of good things that have been brought my way. My grandparents, parents, husband, children, grandkids and great grandkids. I love them all and have enjoyed all they have accomplished in their own lives and families. With these warm thoughts I can say good night and my prayers, now I lay me down to sleep I pray the lord my soul to keep…

www.ingramcontent.com/pod-product-compliance
Lightning Source LLC
LaVergne TN
LVHW020431080526
838202LV00055B/5123